Task Design
and
Employee Motivation

DATE DUE

Management Applications Series

Alan C. Filley, University of Wisconsin, Madison
Series Editor

Performance in Organizations: Determinants and Appraisal
L. L. Cummings, University of Wisconsin, Madison
Donald P. Schwab, University of Wisconsin, Madison

Leadership and Effective Management
Fred E. Fiedler, University of Washington
Martin M. Chemers, University of Utah

Managing by Objectives
Anthony P. Raia, University of California, Los Angeles

Organizational Change: Techniques and Applications
Newton Margulies, University of California, Irvine
John C. Wallace, University of California, Irvine

Interpersonal Conflict Resolution
Alan C. Filley, University of Wisconsin, Madison

*Group Techniques for Program Planning: A Guide to Nominal Group
and Delphi Processes*
Andre L. Delbecq, University of Wisconsin, Madison
Andrew H. Van de Ven, Kent State University
David H. Gustafson, University of Wisconsin, Madison

Organizational Behavior Modification
Fred Luthans, University of Nebraska, Lincoln
Robert Kreitner, Western Illinois University

Task Design and Employee Motivation
Ramon J. Aldag, University of Wisconsin, Madison
Arthur P. Brief, University of Iowa

*Organizational Surveys: An Internal Assessment of Organizational
Health*
Randall B. Dunham, University of Wisconsin, Madison
Frank J. Smith, Sears, Roebuck and Company

Task Design
and
Employee Motivation

Ramon J. Aldag
University of Wisconsin, Madison

Arthur P. Brief
University of Iowa

Scott, Foresman and Company   Glenview, Illinois
Dallas, Tex.   Oakland, N.J.   Palo Alto, Cal.
Tucker, Ga.   London, England

To Our Parents,
Joyce and Melvin Aldag
Lilian and Nat Brief

Library of Congress Cataloging in Publication Data

Aldag, Ramon J   1945-
Task design and employee motivation.

(Management applications series)
Includes bibliographies and index.
1. Job analysis. 2. Work design. 3. Employee motivation. I. Brief, Arthur P.,
1946-   joint author. II. Title.
HF5549.5.J6A56   658.3'06   78-14422
ISBN 0-673-15146-8

THE AUTHORS GRATEFULLY ACKNOWLEDGE PERMISSION TO RE-
PRINT THE FOLLOWING QUOTES AND ILLUSTRATIVE MATERIALS IN
THE TEXT:

P. 41: From *Men, Management, and Morality: Toward a New Organizational Ethic* by
R. T. Golembiewski. Copyright © 1965 by McGraw-Hill, Inc. Used with permis-
sion of McGraw-Hill Book Company. Table 2-1: Reprinted by permission. Table
2-2: Reprinted by permission. Figure 3-1: Copyright 1968 by the American
Psychological Association. Reprinted by permission. Figure 3-2: Reprinted by
permission. Table 3-1: Reprinted by permission. Figure 4-3: Reprinted by per-
mission. Table 4-3: Copyright 1972 by the American Psychological Association.
Reprinted by permission. Table 4-4: Copyright 1972 by the American
Psychological Association. Reprinted by permission. Table 5-1: Copyright 1969
by the American Psychological Association. Reprinted by permission. Table 5-2:
Reprinted by permission. Table 6-1: From T. Burns and G. M. Stalker, *The
Management of Innovation,* published by Tavistock Publications Ltd. Reprinted by
permission. Table 6-2: Jay W. Lorsch and Paul R. Lawrence, eds., *Studies in
Organization Design* (Homewood, Ill.: Richard D. Irwin, Inc. © 1970), p. 95. Re-
printed by permission. Table 6-3: Reprinted by permission. Figure 6-2: Re-
printed by permission. Figure 6-3: Reprinted by permission. Table 6-4: Re-
printed by permission. Figure 7-1: Koch and Fox, *Industrial Relations Research
Association Series,* Madison: Industrial Relations Research Association, 1978,
386-393. Reprinted by permission. Copyright © 1977 by University of Oregon.

2 3 4 5 6 - EBI - 83 82 81 80 79

Foreword

The Management Applications Series is concerned with the application of contemporary research, theory, and techniques. There are many excellent books at advanced levels of knowledge, but there are few which address themselves to the application of such knowledge. The authors in this series are uniquely qualified for this purpose, since they are all scholars who have experience in implementing change in real organizations through the methods they write about.

Each book treats a single topic in depth. Where the choice is between presenting many approaches briefly or a single approach thoroughly, we have opted for the latter. Thus, after reading the book, the student or practitioner should know how to apply the methodology described.

Selection of topics for the series was guided by contemporary relevance to management practice, and by the availability of an author qualified as an expert, yet able to write at a basic level of understanding. No attempt is made to cover all management methods, nor is any sequence implied in the series, although the books do complement one another. For example, change methods might fit well with managing by objectives.

The books in this series may be used in several ways. They may be used to supplement textbooks in basic courses on management, organizational behavior, personnel, or industrial psychology/sociology. Students appreciate the fact that the material is immediately applicable. Practicing managers will want to use individual books to increase their skills, either through self study or in connection with management development programs, inside or outside the organization.

Alan C. Filley

Preface

This book is addressed to practicing managers and to those aspiring to be managers in either public or private sector organizations. The book is intended to serve as a source of ideas which can be put to use as human resource management tools. In addition, we hope it will cause the reader to reflect on the complex interrelationships among the quality of working life, organizational effectiveness, and the responsibilities of management. It is our contention that the content of an employee's job can be a source of personal satisfaction as well as an organizational vehicle to increased employee motivation. The book can be judged on the basis of the degree to which the reader becomes convinced that our contention is valid.

We would like to thank Alan Filley of the University of Wisconsin and Bruce Borland of Scott, Foresman and Company for the opportunity to solidify our thoughts about job design in book form. In addition, we are indebted to Holly Jellinek and Kay and Laura Brief for tolerating the experience of living with "workaholics." Finally, we are appreciative of the editorial assistance of Dane Tyson at Scott, Foresman and the secretarial staffs of the Graduate School of Business, University of Wisconsin—Madison, and the College of Business Administration, The University of Iowa.

Ramon J. Aldag
Madison, Wisconsin

Arthur P. Brief
Iowa City, Iowa

November, 1978

Contents

1　　*Introduction*　　*1*

Some Caveats　　3
The Design of the Book　　4
References　　5

2　　*Essential Employee Behaviors*　　8

Employee Needs　　9
Specific Work Outcomes　　11
Employee Motivation and Job Performance:
　　A Model　　17
Specific Sources of Employee Motivation　　21
Nonmotivational Factors and Performance　　23
Measuring Job Performance　　25
A Noncognitive Approach to Motivation　　27
Summary　　29
References　　30

3　　*Past Perspectives on Job Design*　　34

Work and the Worker: A Historical Overview　　36
Early Approaches to Job Design　　38
Job Enlargement　　42
Job Enrichment　　43
The Task Attributes Literature　　45
Summary　　50
References　　51

4　　*Job Design and Employee Motivation:*
　　A Synthesis　　59

How to Redesign Jobs　　62
Objective Job Characteristics　　70
Summary　　75
References　　77

5   *Individual and Situational Factors in Job Redesign*   81

Urbanization   83
Adherence to Protestant Work Ethic   85
Higher-Order Need Strength   87
Sex, Race, and Age   89
Perceptions of Objective Task Characteristics   93
Physical Characteristics and Physiological
      Responses   95
Situational Factors   98
Summary   100
References   101

6   *Organizational Factors in Job Redesign*   106

Organization Design   108
Technology   119
The Subunit   122
Summary   123
References   123

7   *The Changing Role of the Worker*   127

The Situation in Sweden   131
Developments in the United States   135
Lessons of World Experience   139
Summary   141
References   141

8   *Summary*   143

Index   147

Introduction 1

> *To be a manager requires more than a title, a big office, and other outward symbols of rank. It requires competence and performance of a high order. But does the job demand genius? Is it done by intuition or by method? How does the manager do his work?*
>
> *A manager has two specific tasks. The first is creation of a true whole that is larger than the sum of its parts, a productive entity that turns out more than the sum of the resources put into it. One analogy is the conductor of a symphony orchestra, through whose effort, vision, and leadership individual instrumental parts become the living whole of a musical performance. But the conductor has the composer's score; he is only interpreter. The manager is both composer and conductor.*
>
> *This task requires the manager to make effective whatever strength there is in his resources—above all, in the human resources—and neutralize whatever there is of weakness. This is the only way in which a genuine whole can be created. (Drucker, 1974, p. 398).*

The above quote from Peter F. Drucker's *Management: Tasks, Responsibilities, Practices* likens the job of a manager to that of a composer *and* a conductor. More precise descriptions of managerial work have been offered by several other students of management.[1] Regardless of the description used, a consistently identified aspect of the manager's job concerns the effective utilization of the organization's *human resources*. For instance, Mintzberg (1973) recently described the manager's job in terms of ten roles: figurehead, leader, liaison, monitor, disseminator, spokesman, entrepreneur, disturbance handler, resource allocator, and negotiator. He states that "the *leader* role is clearly the most significant of all roles" (p. 61). According to Mintzberg, the principal purpose of the leader role is to effect an integration between individual needs and organizational goals. Such an integration requires the manager to engage in motivational activities, because an employee's motivation influences what tasks the employee chooses to engage in, how much effort is exerted on those tasks, and for how long a time period that effort will be exerted (cf. Campbell and Pritchard, 1976). Thus, motivation concerns the direction, amplitude, and persistence of an employee's behavior. Obviously, the manager's attainment of organizational goals requires some degree of control over subordinates' motivation. One means of gaining a degree of such control is for the manager to try to satisfy subordinates' needs when they engage in those behaviors which facilitate the attainment of the organization's goals.

Various branches of the social sciences—particularly organizational behavior, psychology, and sociology—offer the serious student of management a wealth of knowledge to aid in understanding, predicting, and controlling employee motivation. This book will draw upon the literatures of these sciences and upon other sources in order to explicate how a manager should go about motivating employees. It is not our purpose to cover a wide array of motivational approaches; rather, we will focus upon employee motivation through job redesign strategies.[2] In other words, this book is principally concerned with how managers might alter the content of their employees' jobs for the purpose of

[1]*For descriptions of managerial work, see Andersson and Nilsson (1964); Burns (1954, 1957); Brewer and Tomlinson (1964); Carlson (1951); Dubin and Spray (1964); Fleishman (1953); Hemphill (1959, 1960); Horne and Lupton (1965); Kay (1959); Kelly (1964); Lawler, Porter, and Tennenbaum (1968); Landsberger (1962); Martin (1956); Mintzberg (1973); O'Neill and Kubany (1959); Ponder (1957); Porter and Ghiselli (1957); Roach (1956); Stewart (1967); Thomason (1966, 1967); and Williams (1956).*
[2]*For a more general treatment of employee motivation, see Campbell and Pritchard (1976); Korman (1974); Lawler (1973); Steers and Porter (1975); and Vroom (1964).*

increasing their desire to achieve the organization's goals. This job redesign approach not only enhances organizational effectiveness but also serves as a means of improving the quality of life for those employees affected by the program.[3] Thus, there may be humanistic as well as economic reasons for pursuing a job redesign intervention.

SOME CAVEATS

A number of guidelines were employed in writing this book. First, within limits, theories of human behavior are presented as the core material in each chapter.[4] All too frequently, people respond negatively to the term "theory," assuming that it refers to the unfounded, impractical speculations of cloistered academicians. Regrettably, in some instances they are right. Every attempt was made, however, to select those theories for presentation which could serve as a practical guide for the manager.

In addition and as noted, the theories introduced have been judged to be acceptable according to five criteria (Filley and House, 1969): (1) Internal consistency—the theory's propositions must be logically structured and free from contradictions; (2) External consistency—the theory must be consistent with observations of real life; (3) Testability—the theory must be clearly and precisely presented so as to allow it to be tested; (4) Wide applicability—the theory must be capable of explaining more than specific, isolated incidents; and (5) Parsimony—the theory should be only as complex as required.

A second guideline employed in writing this book was not to burden the reader with an exhaustive review of research findings pertinent to a particular theoretical model. Rather, research findings have been summarized in the text, and the research literature per se has been extensively referenced, usually in footnotes. These references should be viewed as a relatively comprehensive list of sources to be used by those students who wish to explore a particular issue in greater depth.

[3] *See Bluestone (1974); Davis, Cherns, and Associates (1975); Fein (1973); Hackman and Lawler (1971); Sheppard and Herrick (1972); Walton (1972, 1973); and Work in America (1972).*
[4] *A theory can be thought of as a set of interrelated propositions, and a proposition as a provisional statement which makes predictions about observable phenomena (Filley and House, 1969).*

The third and final guideline relied upon was that the book be as pragmatic as possible. To this end, managerial prescriptions are offered at those points in the text where the level of theoretical development warrants such extensions. Collectively, these prescriptions should serve as an aid to those managers who wish to design and implement effective job redesign interventions.

THE DESIGN OF THE BOOK

The remainder of this text consists of seven chapters. Chapter 2, "Essential Employee Behaviors," explores the behavioral backgrounds to the issue of job redesign, focusing upon employee need structures, motivation, and performance. After presenting a theoretical categorization of employee needs, we closely examine a small subset of the inducements offered by organizations to their employees to remain in the organization and perform their roles. We then introduce a theoretical model of employee motivation based on the assumption that the employee is a rational decision-maker and attempt to demonstrate the role of job redesign in increasing employee motivation and thus raising performance levels.

Chapter 3, "Past Perspectives on Job Design," explores the historical backgrounds of the job design issue. After briefly reviewing the history of work and of attitudes toward it, we focus upon such modern approaches to job design as scientific management, job enlargement, and job enrichment. We then look closely at the recent task attributes literature and explore its relevance to job design.

Chapter 4, "Job Design and Employee Motivation: A Synthesis," is the heart of the book. Here we offer a synthesized theory of job redesign based upon a set of five specific task attributes which represent the most important dimensions of a job. In order to guide managers in applying this theory, we have also spelled out in this chapter an eight-step strategy for the development of a job redesign intervention.

Chapter 5, "Individual and Situational Factors in Job Redesign," recognizes the simple fact that not all employees respond in a like manner to job redesign interventions. Managers must therefore attempt to measure directly employees' preferences for various job characteristics and base their predictions about the likelihood of a successful intervention upon these measurements. The chapter discusses a number of satisfactory and unsatisfactory tools for making such measurements, and examines additional situational factors which must be considered.

Chapter 6, "Organizational Factors in Job Redesign," presents compelling evidence that job redesign efforts should not be attempted without a serious assessment of the organizational context of the target jobs. In particular, we suggest that attention be given to the structure of the aggregate organization and the basic technology used by the organization. Given certain organizational structures and technologies, managers are warned to be cautious of attempting job redesign interventions.

Chapter 7, "The Changing Role of the Worker," is clearly futuristic in its approach. We look first from an international perspective at the current status of worker participation in technical, managerial, and institutional decision-making, focusing upon recent Swedish experiments and the West German model of *codetermination*. We then examine the worker participation movement in the United States and the prospects for increased worker involvement in American and multinational firms.

Chapter 8 offers a brief summary of the major issues explored in the book. Again, the purpose of this book is to offer practicing and potential managers a theoretically sound body of information that will prove useful in fulfilling their job responsibilities. Ideally, the prescriptions provided will also enhance the quality of working life for the subordinates of those managers.

REFERENCES

Andersson, B., and Nilsson, S. Studies in the reliability and validity of the critical incident technique. *Journal of Applied Psychology, 48,* 1964, 398–413.

Bluestone, I. Comments on job enrichment. *Organizational Dynamics, 2,* 1974, 46–47.

Brewer, E., and Tomlinson, J. W. C. The manager's working day. *The Journal of Industrial Economics, 12,* 1964, 191–97.

Burns, T. The directions of activity and communication in a departmental executive group. *Human Relations, 7,* 1954, 73-97.

Burns, T. Management in action. *Operational Research Quarterly, 8,* 1957, 45-60.

Campbell, J. P., and Pritchard, R. D. Motivation theory in industrial and organizational psychology. In *Handbook of Industrial and Organizational Psychology,* ed. by M. D. Dunnette. Chicago: Rand McNally, 1976.

Carlson, S. *Executive Behaviour: A Study of the Work Load and the Working Methods of Managing Directors.* Stockholm: Strombergs, 1951.

Davis, L. E., Cherns, A. B., and Associates. *The Quality of Working Life.* New York: The Free Press, 1975.

Drucker, P. F. *Management: Tasks, Responsibilities, Practices.* New York: Harper & Row, 1974.

Dubin, R., and Spray, S. L. Executive behavior and interaction. *Industrial Relations, 3,* 1964, 99-108.

Fein, M. The real needs and goals of blue-collar workers. *The Conference Board Record, 10,* 1973, 26-33.

Filley, A. C., and House, R. J. *Managerial Process and Organizational Behavior.* Glenview, Ill.: Scott, Foresman, 1969.

Fleishman, E. A. The description of supervisory behavior. *Journal of Applied Psychology, 37,* 1953, 1-6.

Hackman, J. R., and Lawler, E. E., III. Employee reactions to job characteristics. *Journal of Applied Psychology Monograph, 55,* 1971, 259-86.

Hemphill, J. K. Job descriptions for executives. *Harvard Business Review, 37,* 1959, 55-67.

Hemphill, J. K. *Dimensions of Executive Positions.* Columbus: Ohio State University, Bureau of Business Research, Research Monograph Number 98, 1960.

Horne, J. H., and Lupton, T. The work activities of middle managers—An exploratory study. *The Journal of Management Studies, 2,* 1965, 14-33.

Kay, B. R. Key factors in effective foreman behavior. *Personnel, 36,* 1959, 25-31.

Kelly, J. The study of executive behavior by activity sampling. *Human Relations, 17,* 1964, 277-87.

Korman, A. K. *The Psychology of Motivation.* Englewood Cliffs, N.J.: Prentice-Hall, 1974.

Landsberger, H. A. The horizontal dimension in bureaucracy. *Administrative Science Quarterly, 6,* 1962, 299-332.

Lawler, E. E., III. *Motivation in Work Organizations.* Monterey, Calif.: Brooks /Cole, 1973.

Lawler, E. E., III., Porter, L. W., and Tennenbaum, A. Managers' attitudes toward interaction episodes. *Journal of Applied Psychology, 52,* 1968, 432-39.

Martin, N. H. Differential decisions in the management of an industrial plant. *Journal of Business, 29,* 1956, 249-60.

Mintzberg, H. *The Nature of Managerial Work.* New York: Harper & Row, 1973.

O'Neill, H. E., and Kubany, A. J. Observation methodology and supervisory behavior. *Personnel Psychology, 12,* 1959, 85-95.

Ponder, Q. D. The effective manufacturing foreman. In *Industrial Relations Research Association Proceedings of the Tenth Annual Meeting,* ed. by E. Young. Madison, Wis., 1957.

Porter, L. W., and Ghiselli, E. E. The self-perceptions of top and middle management personnel. *Personnel Psychology, 10,* 1957, 397-406.

Roach, D. E. Factor analysis of rated supervisory behavior. *Personnel Psychology, 9,* 1956, 487-98.

Sheppard, H. L., and Herrick, N. *Where Have All the Robots Gone?* New York: The Free Press, 1972.

Steers, R. M., and Porter, L. W. *Motivation and Work Behavior.* New York: McGraw-Hill, 1975.

Stewart, R. *Managers and Their Jobs.* London: Macmillan, 1967.

Thomason, G. F. Managerial work roles and relationships. Part I. *The Journal of Management Studies, 3,* 1966, 270-84.

Thomason, G. F. Managerial work roles and relationships. Part II. *The Journal of Management Studies, 4,* 1967, 17-30.

Vroom, V. H. *Work and Motivation.* New York: Wiley, 1964.

Walton, R. E. How to counter alienation in the plant. *Harvard Business Review, 50,* 1972, 70-81.

Walton, R. E. Quality of working life: What is it? *Sloan Management Review, 15,* 1973, 11-21.

Williams, R. E. A description of some executive abilities by means of the critical incident technique. Ph.D. dissertation, Columbia University, 1956.

Work in America. Report of Special Task Force to Secretary of Health, Education, and Welfare. Washington, D.C.: U.S. Government Printing Office, 1972.

Essential Employee Behaviors

2

Recently, Dr. Abraham Smith, a pediatrician, was overheard saying, "I make twice the money my family needs, but I really feel my patients need me. That's why my case load is so damn heavy."

Judge Jones was complaining about her high cost of living. "My salary barely covers the essentials for me. I was making almost twenty-five thousand dollars more a year in private practice, but I guess being a judge has other rewards. People respect me more. I feel like a role model for younger women."

Ray Brown, talking to his son about his job as an auto mechanic, stated, "Sure, I'll never get rich and I come home from work dirty and tired, but a man has got to enjoy what he's doing. And I sure take pride in listening to an engine I've fine-tuned."

Holly Harris, a production-line employee for a small appliance manufacturer, thought to herself on a recent payday, "If it wasn't for this check, I'd just up and quit that job. The work is so boring that the only way I can keep my sanity is by singing to myself all day."

All of the above individuals are telling us something about

the reasons they work. None of us work for any one reason; different people work for different collections of reasons. An understanding of the needs and desires people hope their work will fulfill for them is essential to successful job design and employee motivation. Knowing what people want out of their work will help you design jobs, compensation systems, and other reward structures in such a way that both the employee and the organization are satisfied.

This chapter will concern a set of concepts basic to the understanding and successful implementation of job redesign: the concepts of needs, performance, and motivation. We will begin by briefly examining the notion of needs and will explore in some detail the specific work outcomes that employees expect to receive from their jobs, and hence the reasons that they work. This first section of the chapter will thus address one basic type of behavior essential for the functioning of any work organization—inducing people to enter and remain within the organization (Katz, 1964).

But mere maintenance of an organization's membership is hardly a sufficient goal for an effective management. A good manager must be equally concerned with achieving the highest levels of performance from employees. The second half of this chapter will thus address another basic type of behavior essential for the functioning of any work organization—motivating employees to carry out their roles in a dependable fashion. As a foundation for this discussion, we will present a detailed model of employee motivation based upon the notion of the employee as a rational decision-maker. We will then examine the sources of intrinsic and extrinsic motivation which can be used by managers to improve employees' job performance, the nonmotivational factors which influence job performance, and the problems inherent in measuring performance. The final section of the chapter will offer an alternative, purely behavioral explanation for variations in employee performance.

EMPLOYEE NEEDS

Probably the best-known theory of human needs was advanced by the late clinical psychologist, Abraham Maslow (1943).

He postulated that people possess the following five prepotent needs, arranged in a hierarchy from lowest to highest:

    1. "Physiological" needs—the need for food, water, air, and sex;
    2. Safety—the need to be free from the threat of bodily harm, i.e., the need for security;
    3. Belongingness—the need for friendship, affection, and love;
    4. Esteem—the need for a feeling of self-worth and for respect and admiration from others;
    5. Self-actualization—the need to make the most of one's life, i.e., the need to obtain self-fulfillment.

According to Maslow, a person must partially fulfill a lower-order need prior to experiencing the next higher need. Since a lower-order need must only be *partially* fulfilled prior to the activation of the next higher need, more than one need can be experienced simultaneously.

The importance of Maslow's work lies in the assertion that people are motivated to engage in those behaviors which they perceive to be a means of fulfilling their experienced needs. People behave to fulfill first lower-order, then higher-order needs, and more than one need can be the focus of a given behavior. Even though Maslow's theory is quite popular as well as intuitively appealing, it has not withstood the rigor of empirical assessment (cf. Wahba and Bridwell, 1976). For example, Hall and Nougaim (1968), in a study of a group of managers employed by American Telephone and Telegraph, found no support for the existence of five distinct categories of needs or for a hierarchy as described by Maslow.

Many other students of human behavior have offered need theories. One potentially useful theory has been advanced by Alderfer (1972). He considers the individual to have three basic sets of needs:

    1. Existence—the need for material existence goods such as food, water, pay, and fringe benefits;
    2. Relatedness—the need for maintaining interpersonal relationships with friends, family, supervisors, co-workers, and subordinates;
    3. Growth—the need for personal development, i.e.,

the need to enhance one's creative or productive potential.

Unlike Maslow's theory which essentially deals with progression up a hierarchy, Alderfer's theory explicitly recognizes the potential for frustration and regression. For example, he proposes that if one's attempts to fulfill growth needs prove to be frustrating, then relatedness needs become more important. Thus, Alderfer's theory is much less rigid than Maslow's.

Alderfer's is a relatively new theory of needs. The limited amount of empirical data which thus far is available, however, is strongly supportive of it. At a minimum Alderfer's theory offers the manager a relatively simple framework for understanding the needs and desires of employees and the role these needs may play in the motivational process.

SPECIFIC WORK OUTCOMES

Understanding employee needs can help us to understand employee behaviors. Figure 2—1 depicts how these needs stand behind the behaviors employees choose to engage in on the job, and how such behaviors (e.g., high job performance) are associated with the occurrence of certain outcomes (e.g., a pay raise). These outcomes may in turn serve to satisfy employees' needs. The outcomes employees receive for engaging in job be-

FIGURE 2—1   A Simple Model of Why People Work

haviors may be viewed as the reasons why they work. Five specific outcomes are usually associated with any work role.[1]

Wages

Clearly, a major reason for working is money, but how central a role money actually plays is an important and largely unanswered question. Reviews of various theories of money (e.g., Lawler, 1971; Opsahl and Dunnette, 1966) shed some light on the issue. Following the thinking of Vroom (1964) and Gellerman (1968), it is generally concluded that the most useful perspective for viewing the role of money is as an instrument for gaining other desired outcomes. Money in and of itself is not important; it acquires importance as a means of fulfilling needs.[2]

Money can, for example, buy such material existence goods as food and thus serve to fulfill employees' existence needs. Money can also be a vehicle for fulfilling relatedness needs, as when an employee uses money to purchase theater tickets for an evening out with friends. Finally, if employees view money as a gauge of personal development, it may play a role in the fulfillment of growth needs by serving as a yardstick of personal achievement.

The importance of money should not be overestimated, however. In a recent sample survey of the noninstitutionalized adult population in the United States, subjects were asked, "If you were to get enough money to live as comfortably as you would like for the rest of your life, would you continue to work or would you stop working?" (Davis, 1975). Over 63 percent of the respondents reported they would continue to work. Furthermore, policy studies of the potential impact of a *negative income tax*—federal transfer payments to replace the current welfare system with a guaranteed minimum income for all families—indicate that nonemployment income is indeed a disincentive to work for the heads of some households. Even so, the heads of many poor families prefer to work regardless of the financial incentive not to work (cf. Green and Tella, 1969).

In total, it appears that money is important if the employee

[1]*The framework for this discussion is drawn largely from Vroom (1964).*
[2]*For a consideration of alternative roles of money, see Opsahl and Dunnette (1966).*

views it as a means to some desired end; but money is clearly not the sole vehicle for satisfying all of the employee's needs.

Expenditure of mental or physical energy

The demands of most jobs keep their occupants physically or intellectually active. Such energy expenditure occupies the employee's time and inhibits the onset of idleness and boredom. The housewife and mother whose children are past preschool age may enter the labor force in large part simply to remain active. Thus energy expenditures per se may be an important reason for working. Neuropsychological studies of brain stimulation indicate that, up to a point at least, people respond favorably in terms of both satisfaction and performance to increased *activation levels,* that is, exposure to a greater number of stimuli in a given period of time (Scott, 1966).

The value of energy expenditure depends upon at least two conditions. First, as indicated by the behavior of our hypothetical housewife, the value placed upon energy expenditure is dependent upon one's state of deprivation. The person seeking ways to pass the time will probably place greater value on the energy consumption aspects of a job than the person who cannot find enough hours in a day to meet current responsibilities. Second, early socialization experiences may lead to the valuing of energy consumption. Some children are taught that work is good and important, a fundamental tenet of the Protestant work ethic (Weber, 1930). Such persons as adults are likely to find their central life interest to be their work (Dubin, 1956) and would probably place greater value on the energy consumption aspects of work than those individuals that are said to be *alienated* from the Protestant work ethic. The role of the Protestant work ethic as a factor in employee motivation will be discussed in greater detail in Chapter 5.

Production of goods and services

The energy expended on a job is directed toward the production of some goods or services. This productive function may be an important reason for working. Farmers who feel the crops they produce help to alleviate hunger, physicians who see their purpose as the reduction of pain and suffering, and teachers who see themselves as builders of young minds are all working, in part at least, to produce a valued commodity. The production of such commodities may in fact be a means of fulfilling growth needs.

Obviously, whether this involvement with the production of goods and services is a salient reason for working depends largely upon one's job. If the end product of one's work activities is not viewed as yielding a valued service or product, then the opportunity for the productive function to play an important role is limited; if the end product is a valued commodity, then one's contribution to the production of this commodity may become an important reason for working.

Social interactions

Most work does not take place in total isolation from other people. Thus, work is social. The clerk whose best friend is a co-worker, the salesperson who enjoys meeting new customers, and the production employee who looks forward to Friday night out with workmates all may be working in part because of the social interactions experienced on the job. Clearly, work may be a principal vehicle for fulfilling relatedness needs.

The importance of the social aspects of work is a function of several factors in addition to the employee's need-state. Aside from the fit between the employee's personality and those of fellow workers, the job itself plays a role in the importance of social interactions, since the design of the job determines those social interactions which are permitted and those which are required. Compare the job of an assembly-line worker on a noisy production line with the closest co-worker more than ten feet away to that of a secretary in a small office who interacts freely with co-workers throughout the workday. These two jobs represent opposite ends of a permitted social interaction continuum with the assembly-line employee's permitted interactions characterized as *restricted* and the secretary's as *permissive.* Required interactions are those interpersonal contacts with supervisors, customers, and co-workers that are task relevant, i.e., demanded by the job. These too can vary along a continuum from restricted to permissive.

In short, the importance of social motives for working seems to vary as a function of the employee's relatedness need strength, the fit between the employee's personality and the personalities of co-workers, and the interactions permitted and required by the job.

Social status

Status is simply the ranking of people in a social system. One type of status is *ascribed*, the status a person is born to. Another more germane type of status is *achieved*, the status a person acquires during the course of a lifetime. Even controlling for income, high-status individuals are accorded relatively more respect and greater freedom in their access to activities, people, and information. People who work generally achieve higher status levels than those who do not. Furthermore, status varies directly as a function of the type of job occupied. The prestige (status) scores of several occupations are listed in Table 2—1.

Several factors help to determine the status of a job. William Whyte (1948), in his classic study of the restaurant industry, found that within the kitchens of large restaurants, status among cooks was largely determined by the materials they worked on. Preparers of beef dishes were accorded more status than preparers of chicken dishes, and fish cooks were accorded lower status than chicken cooks. Other determinants of job status include (a) skill or knowledge required to perform the job, (b) rank or hierarchical position in the organization, (c) wages, (d) seniority, and (e) status of associates (Litterer, 1965).

Social status probably plays a role in facilitating the fulfillment of both relatedness and growth needs. As noted, status is related to one's access to people. More precisely, high-status persons receive more communications than low-status persons, and the content of their communications is more positive (cf. Shaw, 1976). Thus one's status may aid in the fulfillment of relatedness needs. And as is the case with money, if the employee views status and the symbols associated with it as a gauge of personal development, then status may also play a role in the fulfillment of growth needs. The centrality of status should thus not be underestimated by the manager.

TABLE 2—1   Prestige Scores of Selected Occupations

Janitor	16
Bartender	20
Baker	34
Restaurant Manager	39
Plumber	41
Typist	41
Advertising Agent	42
Real Estate Agent	44
Insurance Agent	47
Bank Teller	50
Buyer	50
Sales Manager	50
Stock Broker	51
Industrial Engineer	54
Actuary	55
Personnel and Labor Relations Worker	56
Accountant	57
Economist	57
Public Relations Man	57
Registered Nurse	62
Clergyman	69
Psychologist	71
Bank Officer	72
Judge	76
Business and Commerce Professor	78
Physician	82

Adapted from Davis (1975). Higher scores reflect higher status.

It is necessary to note at this point that the notion of needs we have just discussed cannot and should not be regarded as absolute. All employees do not have the same need structure, and thus individuals will differ in their preferences for work outcomes. Furthermore, these preferences will frequently differ *within* the individual over time. In other words, what the youthful worker desires at the beginning of a career will be somewhat different from that same employee's desires in the more mature stages of life. For example, the authors of one study of career stages conclude that from twenty-five to thirty years of age, the employee is concerned with gaining recognition and establishing a place in the organization; from thirty to forty-five, with advancement; and from forty-five to sixty, with career maintenance

(Hall and Nougaim, 1968).[3] On the other hand, Aldag and Brief (1977), in a study of subjects in a variety of jobs, found no consistent pattern of differences between younger and older employees in the strength of their growth needs. Thus, the manager should be relatively cautious in assuming the existence of a particular age-related pattern in preferences for various work outcomes.

Note also that the five categories of work outcomes we have presented thus far by no means represent an exhaustive listing of the potential rewards associated with work. Later in this chapter, we will examine a much broader array of outcomes. The current set of five outcomes, however, may be viewed differently from other work outcomes. One may think of these as a basic set of inducements an organization offers an individual for occupying a job. Managers should ask themselves which inducements they offer to those who occupy jobs under their supervision. If they find that the jobs supervised can be characterized as low in terms of one or more of the five outcomes, then they should not be surprised by the difficulty experienced in attracting and holding employees. Each of the outcomes can, however, be manipulated in varying degrees. Many can be increased through job redesign. In fact, understanding why, when, and how to manipulate various work outcomes is the essence of the remaining chapters in this book.

Before we can go about manipulating these outcomes, however, we must explore the processes the employee goes through in determining the level of effort to be exerted on the job. We turn our attention, then, to the issue of job performance.

EMPLOYEE MOTIVATION AND JOB PERFORMANCE: A MODEL

The chief auditor of a large corporation was complaining to one of the firm's college recruiters about a new employee. "I don't understand these new college graduates. You pay them good money, but they just don't produce. My new assistant auditor,

---

[3]For a detailed discussion of career stages, see Hall (1976).

Alice Brown, comes in fifteen minutes late every other day, spends most of her time in the women's lounge or chatting with the secretaries, and makes so many errors that I have to have someone check all her work. I've tried everything I know to get her to shape up, but nothing succeeds."

The major concern of most managers is their employees' level of job performance. Thus, the manager should not only be interested in *understanding* the causes of employees' performance, as is the case in selection and placement of employees. Ultimately, the manager is also concerned with *controlling* the level of performance. This concern is not Machiavellian: if the manager's own job performance is measured in terms of the productivity of subordinates, as is frequently the case, then a major concern of the manager will be in maximizing the performance levels of those subordinates. In total, we wish not merely to describe why an employee behaves in a certain way, but also to prescribe how that behavior may be altered.[4]

As noted earlier, people work in order to gain outcomes which they believe will fulfill their existence, relatedness, and growth needs. A slight expansion of this simple framework can be used to understand the level of effort an employee exerts on the job. As shown in Figure 2—2, an employee's level of performance is determined by the level of effort exerted, and that effort is a function of motivation. (The role of such factors as employee skill level as determinants of performance will be addressed later.) Following performance certain work outcomes may occur (e.g., pay raise or promotion). These work outcomes in turn may serve to fulfill the employee's needs. Finally, the level of need fulfillment influences motivation.

In order to understand motivation as a rational decision-making process, the definition of three concepts is essential: expectancy, valence, and instrumentality. *Expectancy* is a perceived effort-performance association. More precisely, expectancy is the employee's estimate of whether he or she is capable of achieving some specified performance goal. In the case of a salesperson, for example, one could measure expectancy by asking the employee, "What are the chances in ten of meeting your assigned sales goal for the next season?" A response of one in ten would indicate that

---

[4]*The material for this discussion is drawn largely from Campbell and Pritchard (1976); Campbell, Dunnette, Lawler, and Weick (1971); Graen (1969); Lawler (1971); Porter and Lawler (1968); and Vroom (1964).*

FIGURE 2—2   A Simple Model of Employee Performance

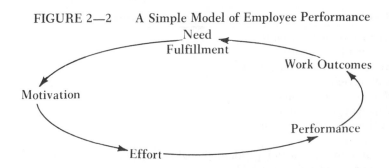

the employee feels that it is highly unlikely that personal effort will lead to the desired level of performance. Conversely, a response of ten in ten would indicate that the employee is certain that effort will lead to the desired performance level. An employee who perceives a low degree of association between personal effort and the resulting level of performance will not be highly motivated to achieve performance goals, since attempts to do so will probably be futile. It is important to note that expectancy, like valence and instrumentality, is based upon the employee's perceptions, which do not necessarily coincide with the reality of the situation. More will be said later about the divergence between employee perception and the objective reality in the workplace.

Valence is the employee's feelings about (i.e., affective orientation toward) a particular work outcome. Valence can be thought of as the level of satisfaction or dissatisfaction an employee expects to experience after attaining a particular work outcome, and can thus be measured in terms of the strength of an employee's desire or aversion for a given outcome. For example, a salesperson may anticipate being promoted from a current sales district to the management of a district located in a distant city. For a career-oriented person, such a promotion may be highly desirable and thus positively valent; for a person with close ties to the current community, such a promotion may be highly aversive and thus negatively valent.

The array of outcomes which may follow an employee's performance could obviously be rather extensive. One list of possible outcomes is presented in Table 2—2. Each manager, however, should attempt to develop a list of outcomes for the unique set of jobs he or she supervises. It is important in determining an

TABLE 2—2   A List of Potential Work Outcomes

Chance to make friends
Respect from co-workers
Being tired from hard work
Giving help to others
Respect from clients
Personal growth and development
Feelings of accomplishment
Pay raise
Greater chance for independent thought and action
Time at work passing quickly
Offering good service
Feelings of security
Promotion
Special awards and recognition
Receiving more compliments
Respect from your boss
Transfer
Being fired
Lowered salary
Becoming bored

Adapted in part from Lawler and Suttle (1971).

employee's level of motivation that the valence of all salient work outcomes be gauged, since the valence of each outcome plays some role in determining motivation. The more positively valent the set of potential outcomes employees anticipate, the more motivated they will be to achieve those outcomes.

Each valence, however, does not contribute independently to motivation. It is weighted by the perceived likelihood that performance will in fact lead to a particular outcome. This perceived performance-outcome association is known as *instrumentality*. The higher the instrumentality, the more weight given to the valence of the outcome, and thus, the more motivation. In short, employees are more highly motivated when they perceive that their performance will lead to desirable work outcomes.

As shown in Figure 2—3, motivation is therefore a function of expectancy multiplied by the sum of the valences for all potential work outcomes, each weighted by its corresponding instrumentality. To increase an employee's motivation, the manager would want to increase the effort-performance linkage (expectancies), the array of outcomes the employee can anticipate as

FIGURE 2—3   The Expectancy Model of Employee Motivation

$$\left[\text{Expectancy} \times \sum(\text{Valence} \times \text{Instrumentality})\right] \xrightarrow{\hspace{2cm}} \text{Effort}$$

being satisfying (valences), and the performance-outcome link-ages (instrumentalities).

The motivational model outlined above has been labeled an *expectancy* or *instrumentality theory of employee motivation*. Several studies offer support for the validity of the model; however, additional research is required to address a number of questions surrounding application of the model.[5] For instance, should the valence of an outcome be measured in terms of the importance or the attractiveness of that outcome to the employee? Nevertheless, the model stands as an extremely useful device for understanding the rational process of employee motivation.

SPECIFIC SOURCES OF EMPLOYEE MOTIVATION

In order to apply practically the model just presented, it is necessary to look more closely at the sources of employee motivation.[6] Two states of motivation, extrinsic and intrinsic, have been identified by researchers. In a state of extrinsic motivation, the employee attributes job behaviors to outcomes which are derived from sources other than the work itself. Such sources could include the employee's co-workers or supervisor, or the organization itself. Examples of extrinsic outcomes could include pay increases, promotions, or fringe benefits. The extrinsically motivated employee tends to feel a lack of control over on-the-job behavior. Examples of employees experiencing a state of extrinsic motivation would include the teacher who states, "Teaching is a bore, but I really enjoy the long Christmas vacations and summers off"; the machinist who states, "My work is awfully dull,

---

[5]*For a review of the research on the expectancy model, see Behling and Starke (1973); Heneman and Schwab (1972); Mitchell (1974); Mitchell and Biglan (1971); Schmidt (1973); and Wahba and House (1974).*
[6]*The following discussion is drawn in part from Brief and Aldag (1977); DeCharms (1968); Deci (1975); and Koch (1956).*

but my company does treat me well"; or the social worker who states, "Dealing with the types of clients I have turns me off, but my work environment is pleasant and my co-workers are interesting and friendly."

In a state of intrinsic motivation, the employee attributes job behaviors to outcomes which are derived from the work itself. Such intrinsic outcomes are experienced by employees independent of the involvement of others, except in those instances where the work involves processing or serving other persons, as is the case with counselors, police officers, and physicians. An employee experiencing a state of intrinsic motivation tends to be committed to the job and self-fulfilled through it. Examples of employees experiencing a state of intrinsic motivation would include the teacher who states, "The money I earn as a teacher is nothing, but I really enjoy introducing a student to a new idea"; the machinist who states, "The company doesn't give me a damn thing, but I take pride in producing a quality product"; or the social worker who states, "My working conditions are horrible and my co-workers are dull, but I get a real sense of satisfaction out of helping my clients."

Clearly, one major means of increasing an employee's level of intrinsic motivation is through changing the work itself, i.e., through redesigning the job. Job redesign for the purpose of increasing motivation (and ultimately performance) essentially requires that the job be restructured to include the opportunity for the employee to experience an array of positively valent intrinsic outcomes which depend upon performance. Merely redesigning the job to incorporate intrinsic outcomes which are *not* contingent upon the employee's performance will probably lead to higher levels of job satisfaction but not necessarily to higher levels of job performance. In other words, an employee will be more satisfied after experiencing an intrinsic outcome; however, based upon the expectancy model of motivation, the employee must perceive that performance leads to such an outcome in order for the anticipation of the outcome to have an effect on the amount of effort exerted. This is why the valence of an outcome is weighted by its corresponding instrumentality. The failure of job redesign programs which increase satisfaction but not performance can thus be explained by the employee's experiencing intrinsic outcomes which are not contingent upon performance. Such is the case when an employee who thoroughly enjoys a job is not very effective at it.

A potentially important exception to the contingency argument concerns task persistence. Several studies have shown that persons performing intrinsically motivating tasks engage in those tasks for longer periods of time than do persons whose tasks are not intrinsically motivating (cf. Deci, 1975). Therefore, in those instances where the employee has discretion over the time devoted to a task, and task persistence leads to greater productivity, one would expect levels of intrinsic motivation to be positively associated with job performance.

The above discussion highlights the position of job satisfaction in the expectancy model. Satisfaction is partially determined by the employee's level of performance. The employee does a good job and is rewarded for it. The employee then derives satisfaction from these performance-contingent rewards. Some students of employee behavior, most notably Frederick Herzberg (1976), argue that satisfaction causes performance (as might be the case with task persistence). But based upon the accumulated empirical evidence, it appears that the relationship depicted in the expectancy model is the most viable.[7] Thus, one should not generally assume that making an employee happy will in turn make the employee productive.

NONMOTIVATIONAL FACTORS AND PERFORMANCE

As noted, an employee's level of motivation determines the amount of effort exerted on the job. As shown in Figure 2—4, whether in fact this effort influences performance is dependent upon at least three additional factors: the aptitudes, skills, and abilities of the employee, the employee's role perceptions, and the technology employed on the job.[8]

Aptitudes, skills, and *abilities* are the cognitive, motor, and physical proficiency attributes which enable an employee to perform a job well.[9] One list of such attributes includes verbal

[7]*For reviews of the research on performance-satisfaction relationships, see Organ (1977) and Schwab and Cummings (1970).*
[8]*The material for this discussion is drawn in part from Lawler (1971) and Porter and Lawler (1968).*
[9]*For a detailed discussion of how tests of such attributes can be used in the selection and placement of employees, see Dunnette (1966, 1976); Guion (1976); and Schneider (1976).*

FIGURE 2—4   The Effort-Performance Relationship

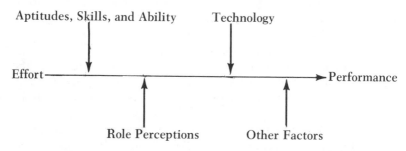

comprehension, numerical ability, visual pursuit, visual accuracy, space visualization, numerical reasoning, verbal reasoning, word fluency, manual speed and accuracy, and symbolic reasoning (Ruch and Ruch, 1963). Although an employee may be highly motivated and thus exert high levels of effort on the job, this effort may not translate into high levels of performance because of a lack of the appropriate aptitude, skill, or ability. Such would be the case, for example, with a highly motivated secretary who could type only twenty-five words per minute.

Role perceptions refer to how the employee defines the job, and to the direction, rather than the level, of effort the employee believes is essential to effective job performance. Again, the highly motivated employee's effort may not translate into high performance because of an incongruence between the employee's and the organization's definition of the job. For example, one of the authors as the manager of a men's clothing store supervised a highly energetic salesperson; but although his main duty was to wait on customers and sell clothes, the salesperson spent all of his time straightening the stock and keeping the store orderly. Thus, his sales performance was low despite his motivational level. In total, therefore, managers should make sure that employees clearly understand the organization's expectations.

Technology here refers to the operations, materials, and knowledge employed in producing or distributing a good or service (cf. Gillespie and Mileti, 1977; Hickson, Pugh, and Pheysey, 1969). The role of technology is as a variable which changes the nature of the relationship between effort and performance. A production employee who operates a machine which processes a unit every two minutes is constrained by the technology of the job to produce no more than a unit every two minutes. A dentist who requires at least four to five minutes to properly fill a cavity in a tooth is limited by the technology of the profession to processing a limited number of patients in a given day. Technological constraints on performance are indeed obvious, but they need to be identified and recognized as factors which restrict the potential of the employee's motivation.

Other factors which may function as moderators of the effort-performance relationship include such things as market demand and the social structure of the workplace. In regard to market demand, if a production employee is faced with orders for only twenty units in a given day, the employee's productivity will be limited to those twenty units even though actual productive capacity may be twenty-five units. In addition, Collins and Guetzkow (1964) have noted that the energy of any work group is directed toward two activities: maintenance of the group and productivity of the group. Group maintenance activities (e.g., the continuation of pleasant interpersonal relations) may distract from productivity. Thus the social structure of the workplace may also serve as a factor which constrains the motivational potential of the individual.

In sum, it has been suggested that the aptitudes, skills, and role perceptions of an employee, as well as the technology employed on the job and other factors, may reduce or enhance the relationship between an employee's effort and subsequent performance level. Thus, the manager should not expect a one-to-one correspondence between motivation and performance. Rather, the variables identified as influencing the effort-performance relationship should be viewed as potential nonmotivational obstacles to maximum employee performance. These influencing variables could require such managerial interventions as a training program to upgrade employee skills, the establishment of written procedures to clarify role perceptions, or the application of various engineering techniques to the technology employed.

MEASURING JOB PERFORMANCE

Given the centrality of subordinate job performance to a manager, it is surprising to find that in many instances managers seem to avoid any sincere attempt at gauging the performance levels of their subordinates. This may occur for a number of reasons. First, managers may not have the expertise necessary to develop a workable performance appraisal system and thus feel that the performance of their subordinates is too complex to quantify. One frequently hears such an argument from managers who supervise professionals such as accountants, nurses, or market researchers. Second, on an interpersonal level, not measuring performance may be more comfortable for supervisors than measuring performance and being required to feed back negative information to employees. Finally, it may simply be easier not to measure performance: the development of a sound performance appraisal system takes time, effort, and money.

The repercussions of not measuring performance should, however, be obvious. A compensation system which is not backed up by a solid performance appraisal system might permit low-performing employees to receive a higher level of compensation than outstanding performers. In such a situation mediocrity rather than excellence could be rewarded. The discussion to follow, however, assumes that the manager has available hard (i.e., objective) measures of subordinate job performance. A few properties of such performance are noted below.[10]

Job performance is a multidimensional construct which varies along at least two dimensions—quantity and quality of output. Further, job performance varies over time. One's performance at midmorning Wednesday is probably very different than one's performance late Friday afternoon. Some people are most productive in the early morning hours and others in the late evening. Thus, multiple dimensions of job performance should be measured at multiple points in time. A single overall judgment of a subordinate's performance once a year should probably be avoided.

A measure of job performance should be acceptable to those using it, comprehensible to all parties involved, and representative of meaningful behavior on the job. In other words, a good measure of job performance will exhibit a high degree of face validity (i.e., will make intuitive sense to those using the measure), will be easily understood, and will tap those job behaviors that are in fact important to organizational effectiveness.

The very process of appraising employee performance has

[10]*The following discussion is drawn largely from Korman (1971).*

an influence on subsequent employee performance as well as job satisfaction. Thus, care must be taken in designing the social aspects (i.e., the pattern of superior-subordinate interactions) of any performance appraisal system.

Finally, factors other than actual job performance may have an influence on the ratings of a subordinate. Even though employee performance is quantifiable, numerous biases and other sources of error enter into the performance appraisal process. Characteristics of both the supervisor and the employee must be examined as possible sources of trouble, such as, for example, systematic differences in evaluations according to sex, race, or age. The developers of good performance appraisal systems attempt to insulate against such errors.[11]

A NONCOGNITIVE APPROACH TO MOTIVATION

Thus far, the motivational process has been viewed as a decision-making process which takes place within the employee. Before concluding the chapter, a noncognitive, purely behavioral perspective on employee motivation will be introduced. This alternative theory is also supported by considerable research and should be viewed as a competing, yet complementary, perspective.[12]

This alternative model has been labeled *reinforcement* or *learning theory*. Its core contention is that an individual's behavior can best be understood and predicted by examining the consequences of that behavior. Reinforcement theory is concerned with two categories of behavior—*involuntary* or *reflex behaviors* (e.g., dilation of the pupil of the eye in response to a bright light) and *voluntary* or *operant behaviors* (e.g., coming to work on time). Our own interest is solely with the voluntary behaviors of the employee.

To understand an employee's behavior from a reinforcement theory perspective three aspects of that behavior must al-

[11]*For a more in-depth discussion of the measurement of job performance, see Cummings and Schwab (1973).*
[12]*This discussion is drawn in part from Hamner (1974) and Luthans and Kreitner (1975).*

ways be specified: (1) the occasion upon which a behavior occurs, called the *stimulus condition;* (2) the behavior itself, conceptualized as performance; and (3) the performance-contingent reinforcement the employee experiences following the behavior. To change (or modify) an employee's behavior, the manager must alter these reinforcing consequences. Consequences may be manipulated in a number of ways. The manager may, for example, deliver a positive reinforcement (a reward) following a fixed number of desired responses, in the manner of a piece-rate schedule of pay.[13]

It is important to note that the manager should not expect to control the entire array of consequences which occur in the workplace. Co-workers, clients, customers, the work itself, and the individual employee can all exercise a degree of control over consequences. For example, a job which allows the employee to experience a sense of accomplishment can be viewed as positively reinforcing the employee's job behaviors. Thus, the distinction between a positive reinforcement and a positively valent outcome becomes somewhat blurred.[14]

In total, reinforcement theory offers an alternative and useful means of understanding and predicting employee performance. Unlike expectancy theory, it is not dependent upon understanding the internal states of the employee. The application of reinforcement theory to the practice of management is becoming increasingly popular.[15] Nord (1969) describes the use of it in a St. Louis hardware company. Employees who reported to work on time every day for a month became eligible for a twenty-five dollar lottery prize; at the end of six months, people with perfect attendance records became eligible in a drawing for a color television set. After sixteen months of operation, the cost of absenteeism had been reduced by 62 percent.

Such a movement forward should not, however, leave behind the vast body of information that has been accumulated about the thoughts, feelings, and desires of the employee. It appears to the authors that reinforcement theory and the expectancy model are complementary; the manager need not rely

[13]*For detailed discussions of behavior modification, see Bandura (1969) and Tharp and Wetzel (1969).*
[14]*See Scott (1975) for an opposing position.*
[15]*For discussion of the application of reinforcement theory to employee behavior, see Heiman (1975); Jablonsky and DeVries (1972); Mawhinney (1975); Nord (1969); and Yukl and Latham (1975).*

solely upon one perspective but should draw simultaneously upon both (cf. Berger, Cummings, and Heneman, 1975). Successful redesign of jobs requires several conceptual approaches, methodologies, and techniques, the uses of which will be described in later chapters.

SUMMARY

The purpose of this chapter has been to give the reader an understanding of the behavioral questions relevant to the issue of job redesign. We began by discussing employee needs, which may be viewed as falling into one of three categories: *existence, relatedness,* or *growth.* Associated with any work role are certain outcomes which to varying degrees help to fulfill these needs and thus serve as reasons for working. Such outcomes include wages, expenditure of energy, production of valued goods and services, social interaction, and social status.

The *expectancy model of motivation,* which assumes that the employee is a rational decision-maker, can be a useful tool in understanding the relationship between needs, motivation, and performance. According to this model, motivation is a multiplicative function of three variables: *expectancy* (the employee's probability estimate of achieving a performance goal), *valence* (the satisfaction the employee expects to experience from a particular outcome), and *instrumentality* (the employee's belief that performance will lead to that outcome). A manager's manipulation of any of these variables may increase employee motivation.

Motivation may be thought of as either *extrinsic* (derived from sources outside the work itself) or *intrinsic* (derived from the nature of the work itself). Job redesign, by restructuring a particular job to incorporate potential outcomes which the employee regards as valuable, may thus play a major role in increasing intrinsic motivation and hence performance. Several potential moderators of the effort-performance relationship include the employee's aptitudes, abilities, and role perceptions, the technology and social structure of the organization, and even market demand. All these factors may prevent an increase in employee motivation from translating into improved job performance.

Reinforcement theory represents an alternative to the expectancy model in explaining employee behavior. The theory suggests that an employee's behavior may be modified by rewarding or *reinforcing* desired modes of behavior. Unlike the expectancy model, reinforcement theory does not depend upon an understanding of the employee's inner feelings; however, the two theories are not necessarily contradictory, and managers should draw upon both perspectives in redesigning jobs.

REFERENCES

Aldag, R. J., and Brief, A. P. Age, work values, and employee reactions. *Industrial Gerontology, 4,* 1977, 192–97.

Alderfer, C. P. *Existence, Relatedness, and Growth: Human Needs in Organizational Settings.* New York: The Free Press, 1972.

Bandura, A. *Principles of Behavior Modification.* New York: Rinehart and Winston, 1969.

Behling, O., and Starke, F. A. The postulates of expectancy theory. *Academy of Management Journal, 16,* 1973, 373–88.

Berger, C. J., Cummings, L. L., and Heneman, H. G. Expectancy theory and operant conditioning predictions of performance under variable ratio and continuous schedules of reinforcement. *Organizational Behavior and Human Performance, 14,* 1975, 227–43.

Brief, A. P., and Aldag, R. J. The intrinsic extrinsic dichotomy: Toward conceptual clarity. *Academy of Management Review, 2,* 1977, 493–99.

Campbell, J. P., and Pritchard, R. D. Motivation theory in industrial and organizational psychology. In *Handbook of Industrial and Organizational Psychology,* ed. by M. D. Dunnette. Chicago: Rand McNally, 1976.

Campbell, J. P., Dunnette, M. D., Lawler, E. E., and Weick, K. E. *Managerial Behavior, Performance, and Effectiveness.* New York: McGraw-Hill, 1970.

Collins, B. E., and Guekzkow, H. *A Social Psychology of Group Processes for Decision-Making.* New York: Wiley, 1964.

Cummings, L. L., and Schwab, D. P. *Performance in Organizations.* Glenview, Ill.: Scott, Foresman, 1973.

Davis, J. A. *Spring 1975 General Social Survey: National Data Pro-*

gram for the Social Sciences. Ann Arbor: Inter-University Consortium for Political Research, 1975.

Deci, E. L. *Intrinsic Motivation.* New York: Plenum Press, 1975.

DeCharms, R. *Personal Causation.* New York: Academic Press, 1968.

Dubin, R. Industrial workers' world: A study of the "central life interests" of industrial workers. *Social Problems, 3,* 1956, 131–42.

Dunnette, M. D., *Handbook of Industrial and Organizational Psychology.* Chicago: Rand McNally, 1976.

Dunnette, M. D. *Personnel Selection and Placement.* Belmont, Calif.: Wadsworth, 1966.

Gellerman, S. W. *Management by Motivation.* New York: American Management Association, 1968.

Gillespie, D. F., and Mileti, D. S. Technology and the study of organizations: An overview and appraisal. *Academy of Management Review, 2,* 1977, 7–16.

Graen, G. Instrumentality theory of work motivation: Some experimental results and suggested modifications. *Journal of Applied Psychology Monograph, 53,* 1969, 1–25.

Green, C., and Tella, A. Effect of nonemployment income and wage rates on the work incentives of the poor. *Review of Economics and Statistics, 51,* 1969, 399–408.

Guion, R. M. Recruiting, selection and job placement. In *Handbook of Industrial and Organizational Psychology,* ed. by M. D. Dunnette. Chicago: Rand McNally, 1976.

Hall, D. T. *Careers in Organizations.* Pacific Palisades, Calif.: Goodyear, 1976.

Hall, D. T., and Nougaim, K. E. An examination of Maslow's need hierarchy in an organizational setting. *Organizational Behavior and Human Performance, 3,* 1968, 12–35.

Hamner, W. C. Reinforcement theory and contingency management in organizational settings. In *Organizational Behavior and Management: A Contingency Approach,* ed. by H. L. Tosi and W. C. Hamner. Chicago: St. Clair Press, 1974.

Heiman, G. W. A note on "Operant conditioning principles extrapolated to the theory of management." *Organizational Behavior and Human Performance, 13,* 1975, 165–70.

Heneman, H. G., and Schwab, D. P. Evaluation of research on expectancy theory predictions of employee performance. *Psychological Bulletin, 78,* 1972, 1–9.

Herzberg, F. *The Managerial Choice: To Be Efficient and to Be Human.* Homewood, Ill.: Dow Jones-Irwin, 1976.

Hickson, D. J., Pugh, D. S., and Pheysey, D. C. Operations technology and organization structure: An empirical reappraisal. *Administrative Science Quarterly, 14,* 1969, 378–97.

Jablonsky, S. F., and DeVries, D. L. Operant conditioning principles extrapolated to the theory of management. *Organizational Behavior and Human Performance, 7,* 1972, 340–58.

Katz, D. The motivational basis of organizational behavior. *Behavioral Science, 9,* 1964, 131–48.

Koch, S. Behavior as 'intrinsically' regulated: Work notes toward a pretheory of phenomena called motivational. In *Nebraska Symposium on Motivation,* ed. by M. R. Jones. Lincoln, Neb.: University of Nebraska Press, 1956.

Korman, A. K. *Industrial and Organizational Psychology.* Englewood Cliffs, N.J.: Prentice-Hall, 1971.

Lawler, E. E., III. *Pay and Organizational Effectiveness.* New York: McGraw-Hill, 1971.

Lawler, E. E., III, and Suttle, J. L. Expectancy theory and job behavior. *Organizational Behavior and Human Performance, 9,* 1973, 482–503.

Litterer, J. A. *The Analysis of Organizations.* New York: Wiley, 1965.

Luthans, F., and Kreitner, R. *Organizational Behavior Modification.* Glenview, Ill.: Scott, Foresman, 1975.

Maslow, A. H. A theory of human motivation. *Psychological Review, 50,* 1943, 370–96.

Mawhinney, T. C. Operant terms and concepts in the description of individual work behavior: Some problems of interpretation, application, and evaluation. *Journal of Applied Psychology, 60,* 1975, 704–12.

Mitchell, T. R. Expectancy model of job satisfaction, occupational preference, and effort: A theoretical, methodological and empirical appraisal. *Psychological Bulletin, 81,* 1974, 1053–77.

Mitchell, T. R., and Biglan, A. Instrumentality theories: Current uses in psychology. *Psychological Bulletin, 76,* 1971, 432–54.

Nord, W. R. Beyond the teaching machine: The neglected area of operant conditioning in the theory and practice of management. *Organizational Behavior and Human Performance, 4,* 1969, 375–407.

Opsahl, R. L., and Dunnette, M. D. The role of financial compensation in industrial motivation. *Psychological Bulletin, 66,* 1966, 94–118.

Organ, D. W. A reappraisal and reinterpretation of the satisfaction-causes-performance hypothesis. *Academy of Management Review, 2,* 1977, 46–53.

Porter, L. W., and Lawler, E. E., *Managerial Attitudes and Performance.* Homewood, Ill.: Irwin, 1968.

Ruch, F. L., and Ruch, W. W. *Employee Aptitude Survey: Technical Report.* Los Angeles: Psychological Services, 1963.

Schmidt, F. L. Implications of a measurement problem for expectancy theory research. *Organizational Behavior and Human Performance, 10,* 1973, 243–51.

Schwab, D. P., and Cummings, L. L. Theories of performance and satisfaction: A review. *Industrial Relations, 9,* 1970, 408–30.

Scott, W. E. The effects of extrinsic rewards on "intrinsic motivation." *Organizational Behavior and Human Performance, 15,* 1976, 117–29.

Schneider, B. *Staffing Organizations.* Pacific Palisades, Calif.: Goodyear, 1976.

Scott, W. E. Activation theory and task design. *Organizational Behavior and Human Performance, 1,* 1966, 3–30.

Shaw, M. E. *Group Dynamics: The Psychology of Small Groups.* New York: McGraw-Hill, 1976.

Tharp, R. G., and Wetzel, R. J. *Behavior Modification in the Natural Environment.* New York: Academic Press, 1969.

Vroom, V. H. *Work and Motivation.* New York: Wiley, 1964.

Wahba, M. A., and House, R. J. Expectancy theory in work and motivation: Some logical and methodological issues. *Human Relations, 27,* 1974, 121–47.

Wahba, M., and Bridwell, L. Maslow reconsidered: A review of the research on the need hierarchy theory. *Organizational Behavior and Human Performance, 15,* 1976, 212–40.

Weber, M. *The Protestant Ethic and the Spirit of Capitalism.* London: Allen and Unwin, 1930.

Whyte, W. F. *Human Relations in the Restaurant Industry.* New York: McGraw-Hill, 1948.

Yukl, G. A., and Latham, G. P. Consequences of reinforcement schedules and incentive magnitudes for employee performance: Problems encountered in an industrial setting. *Journal of Applied Psychology, 60,* 1975, 294–98.

Past Perspectives 3
on Job Design

The Secretary of Labor, James Hodgson, was on the Today Show this morning. He said that the only two things that workers are interested in are their paychecks and their families.

I think they are also interested in the content of their jobs and about what they do when they go through the plant doors. I think the Secretary has misread what has happened across this land, if he does not understand workers are increasingly dissatisfied by working conditions, even if they are satisfied by their paycheck.

As a nation, we have prided ourselves in the past on the skills and initiative and capacity of the American worker. And we have watched as pay raises and benefits seemed to provide a just recompense for the workers.

But then we stopped looking. We stopped looking at working conditions. We stopped looking at health hazards in the work place. We stopped looking at physical hazards. Only now, with the passage of the Occupational Health and Safety Act of 1970 has there been an expression of national concern.

Now we have stopped looking again. The Nation marvels at the impressive speed of the automated equipment in the Nation's modern plants and assumes that productivity is at an all-time high. Unfortunately, it is as if the Nation's institutions were mesmerized by the industrial machine and unable to see the man behind the machine.

For the key element in the productivity equation is the worker and the noneconomic needs of the worker have been forgotten. Too many young workers are finding their jobs a place of confinement and frustration. And we should not be surprised that our lack of concern is producing a class of angry and rebellious workers.

This year, we have learned in the primaries that millions of Americans are alienated. They are alienated because of the war. They are alienated because they see Government respond to special interests and not the public interest. They are alienated because they see their taxes rise and read about loopholes for corporations and the wealthy.

And we also have learned that millions of Americans are alienated because they see their jobs as dead-ends, monotonous and depressing and without value.

And we in the Congress have a responsibility to see what can be done to end that alienation and to return the sense of excitement and adventure that traditionally has characterized our people.

Few people in America have ever heard of Lordstown, where auto workers have tied up the lines more than once to protest the robot-like monotony of a 36-second interval assembly process.

Fewer of us are aware or can understand the causes why a worker recently went berserk in the Eldon axle plant in Detroit and shot three foremen. His defense was insanity, brought about by working in the noise and filth and danger of that plant. The judge and jury visited the plant and their verdict was unanimous. It was a verdict for acquittal.

That is the extreme. But how many men and women unnecessarily suffer mental or physical illnesses whose cause is linked to their jobs? What is the extent of use of drugs and alcoholism among young workers? How many men and women could function more effectively as parents and citizens if they did not feel dissatisfied with their jobs?

Equally important for the economic vitality of this Nation is the effect that worker discontent has on productivity. The National Commission on Productivity states that in at least one major industry, absenteeism increased by 50 percent, worker turnover by 70 percent, worker grievances by 38 percent, and disciplinary layoffs by 44 percent in a period of 5 years. How much does that cost the economy in terms of lost time, in terms of retraining new workers, in terms of low productivity? (Kennedy, 1972).

Senator Edward Kennedy's 1972 statement to the Senate's Subcommittee on Employment, Manpower, and Poverty asserts that job content (i.e., the work itself) and the quality of working life are intimately linked,[1] and that a low quality of working life could be associated with a variety of social ills, as well as with reduced productivity. Although this book deals more with the relationship between job design and organizationally relevant outcomes (i.e., employee satisfaction and performance) than with larger social questions, Senator Kennedy's statement accurately emphasizes an issue which the reader should keep in mind: the importance of job design to society as a whole.

In this chapter, we explore how the situation of workers came to be the way Kennedy describes it, and some of the remedies that have been proposed and attempted in this century. We begin with a brief historical sketch of the notion of work and of attitudes toward it, in order to place the concept of job design in perspective. We then examine various approaches to job design dating from the industrial revolution to the present, including job enlargement, job enrichment, and other contemporary approaches to the problem. The chapter closes with a review of recent literature dealing with specific task attributes.

WORK AND THE WORKER: A HISTORICAL OVERVIEW

The modern attitude toward work is in fact the product of an evolutionary process which dates back to the very beginnings of human history.[2] In precivilized times, the concept of work per se did not exist: individuals in primitive societies took their food and shelter when and where they found them, and in retrospect, it is difficult to draw any distinction between their work and leisure activities. As plants and animals became domesticated, however, populations grew rapidly, encouraging the development of technology and a social definition of work, with the lowest classes being assigned the most physically demanding labor.

[1]For discussions concerning the definition and importance of the "quality of working life" construct, see Davis, Cherns, and Associates (1975); Macy and Mirvis (1976); Sheppard and Herrick (1972); Work in America (1972); and Walton (1973).
[2]Portions of this discussion are drawn from Dubin (1976); George (1968); Heneman (1973); and Parker and Smith (1976).

The ancient Greeks and Romans viewed work as a curse and nothing more (Mills, 1956; Tilgher, 1931). Work was performed largely by slaves, and the leisure time reserved for the upper classes allowed them to exercise mind and spirit in the consideration of truth and virtue. The Hebrews viewed work much as did the Greeks and Romans, but added the belief that work was a product of original sin and a vehicle for atonement. Thus the Hebrews were among the first peoples to see work in something of a positive light. As the atonement of sin, work was a means of cooperating with God in the world's salvation.

Early Christians largely adopted this Hebrew perspective on work. In addition, however, they felt that work could generate a surplus of goods and services to be shared with the poor. But although the early Christians saw work as generating the opportunity to be charitable, they, like their ancestors, recognized little intrinsic value in work. Because the fruits of work could only be enjoyed in this life, the early Catholic Church did not emphasize the role of work in its teachings. Though work was seen as natural, nonwork held a higher status, since in lieu of work, one could pray and contemplate the spiritual life.

An abrupt change, however, occurred in Christian teachings with the writings of Luther. He taught that the best way to serve God was to excel in one's chosen vocation. Through Luther, work came to be valued as a path to salvation. Calvin developed this idea further, arguing that work was the will of God and that the accumulation of personal wealth was a sign of virtue. But Calvin insisted that this wealth should be shared with the poor and not used as a source of personal pleasure. These teachings were the foundation of what is known today as the "Protestant work ethic."

Since the Renaissance, some have held that creative work could be a joy in itself, void of any religious connotation. The industrial revolution helped to solidify this nonreligious view, as work became the dominant means of acquiring material goods and services. To some degree, however, the notion that certain forms of work may be intrinsically satisfying was retained. Thus arose the modern view of work: work can play a major role in satisfying both the economic and psychological needs of men and women. In this modern view is rooted the current concern with job design.

EARLY APPROACHES TO JOB DESIGN[3]

The industrial revolution, born in Europe during the late 1700s, presented managers with a host of technological and human relations problems never before imagined. Charles Babbage, an Englishman, was probably the first writer to advocate that managers deal with these problems scientifically rather than relying solely upon guesswork, hunches, and intuition (Babbage, 1832). He emphasized the importance of job specialization, claiming that it would reduce labor cost and the time required to learn a job, and would increase the skill level of employees. Babbage stated that:

> ... the master manufacturer, by dividing the work to be executed into different processes, each requiring different degrees of skill and force, can purchase exactly the precise quantity of both which is necessary for each process; whereas, if the whole work were executed by one workman, that person must possess sufficient skill to perform the most difficult, and sufficient strength to execute the most laborious of the operations into which the act is divided (p. v.).

Frederick W. Taylor, however, who began his career in 1878 as a pattern-maker with Midvale Steel Company of Philadelphia, is credited with being the founder of the movement which came to be known as *scientific management* (Taylor, 1903; 1911). Among other things, Taylor's writings dealt with (a) selecting, training, and compensating the employee, (b) designing the employee's job and tools, and (c) assigning management the responsibility for taking *initiative*, which was previously vested with the employee. The exercise of management initiative included gathering together the traditional knowledge possessed by the employee, and classifying, tabulating, and reducing this knowledge to rules and formulae which would lead to absolute uniformity in employee behavior (Taylor, 1911).[4]

[3]*Portions of this discussion are drawn from George (1968); Haimann and Scott (1974); McFarland (1974); and Turner and Lawrence (1965).*
[4]*For a discussion of the current uses of scientific management, see Shapiro and Wahba (1974).*

In the area of job design, Taylor and his associates (e.g., Gilbreth, 1914) advocated that time-and-motion studies be used to determine the one best way of doing a job and that all employees performing the same job be required to use the techniques and procedures so identified. This process of work simplification and standardization was shown to conserve time, money, and energy. These benefits are probably best described by Gilbreth in his *Primer of Scientific Management* (1914):

> ... suppose that under the old plan of management a man turned out about 10 pieces per day and received a total daily wage of $4.00. That would equal forty cents apiece.
>
> Now suppose that by analyzing the methods of making, down to the minutest motions, and by discovering a new method that took less time with less effort and was subject to less delay, the worker was able to put out 25 pieces, for which he received twenty-five cents apiece. The man's pay is here raised more than 56 percent, and the production costs have been lowered 37 1/2 percent ... (p. 20).

> It is the aim of scientific management to induce men to act as nearly like machines as possible, so far as doing the work in the one best way that has been discovered is concerned. After the worker has learned that best way, he will have a starting point from which to measure any new method that his ingenuity can suggest. But until he has studied and mastered the standard method, he is requested not to start a debating society on that subject (p. 50).

> Standardization enables, and offers a constant incentive to, employees to try for better standards, not only for the joy of achieving, but also for the money reward that comes from making a better standard (p. 69).

> The advantage in speed, productivity, and ease of performance that comes from habits of exactly the same sequence of motions and the absence of the mental process of making a complete decision for each motion cannot be appreciated by any one who has not made this subject a life study (p. 75).

Taylor's approach to job design was seen by many as a means of accruing to the organization numerous benefits, including reductions in training cost, labor cost, and worker fatigue, and a simplification of production scheduling (cf. Lawler, 1973). In fact, scientific management is probably one of the major factors contributing to the current level of industrialization. Interestingly enough, however, during the first part of the twentieth century, scientific management was viewed by some as a vehicle for the radical restructuring of contemporary society. A committee of the U.S. Congress even held hearings in 1913 to investigate the potential consequences of Taylor's work (cf. Taylor, 1947).

Paralleling the growth of scientific management was the emergence of industrial psychology (Munsterberg, 1913), which at that time was principally concerned with complementing and extending Taylor's work. Primary concern was focused on selection and on what is now known as the *human engineering* or *human factors* aspects of job and equipment design.

Beginning in the late 1940s, numerous students of employee behavior and attitude from a wide variety of academic disciplines began to question whether or not the cost of work simplification and standardization in terms of job dissatisfaction, absenteeism, and turnover, and the difficulties of effectively managing employees who perceive their jobs as monotonous offset the benefits accrued.[5] The Technology Project of the Institute of Human Relations at Yale University, conducted by Charles Walker and his colleagues (e.g., Guest, 1955; Jasinski, 1956; Turner, 1956; Walker and Guest, 1952; Walker, Guest, and Turner, 1956), exemplifies the programs of research which led to such questioning. For example, Walker and Guest (1952), in a study of over 1000 persons employed in the production of automobiles, found high levels of absenteeism, turnover, and job dissatisfaction among individuals who occupied repetitive, machine-paced jobs.

The consequences associated with "routinization," the re-

[5]This early literature is rather extensive. For example, see Argyris (1957); Bell (1956); Blauner (1964); Davis (1957a, b; 1962); Davis and Canter (1955); Davis, Canter, and Hoffman (1955); Davis and Werling (1960); Gillespie (1948); Guest (1955); Jasinski (1956); Kornhauser (1965); Likert (1961); McGregor (1957); Turner and Miclette (1962); Walker (1950; 1954; 1962); Walker and Guest (1952); and Whyte (1955).

sult of work simplification and standardization, have been summarized as follows (Golembiewski, 1965):

1. The worker loses control, as in being paced by a machine or assembly line.

2. The simplification of work reduces the possibility of the employee developing skills that can lead to his advancement.

3. The simplification of work also depersonalizes work in that skill content tends to be reduced and equalized, thus undermining the hierarchy of skills that (for example) can constitute a promotion ladder and can give social meaning to work.

4. The simplification of work reduces the degree to which the individual can meaningfully participate in organizational affairs through his work.

5. The simplification of work often prevents the individual from completing a task that is meaningful to him.

6. The routinization of work implies monotony.

7. The routinization of work often requires that the individual work alone or, at least, there are few positive incentives for individuals in separate organization units to integrate their contributions into a smooth flow of work (pp. 122–23).

A model reflecting the questions raised about the virtues of simplified, low skill-level, short-cycle jobs is presented in Figure 3—1. In response to these potential negative effects of routine jobs, some researchers in the 1950s began to advocate job redesign in the form of job enlargement.

FIGURE 3—1   The Behavioral Consequences of Work Simplification and Standardization

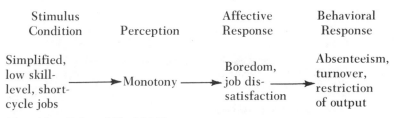

Stimulus Condition	Perception	Affective Response	Behavioral Response
Simplified, low skill-level, short-cycle jobs	Monotony	Boredom, job dis-satisfaction	Absenteeism, turnover, restriction of output

Adapted from Hulin and Blood (1968).

JOB ENLARGEMENT

Job enlargement is defined as "the expansion of job content to include a wider variety of tasks and to increase the worker's freedom of pace, responsibility for checking quality, and discretion for method" (Kilbridge, 1960, p. 357). Specific elements of job enlargement include (a) increasing the number of tasks, (b) increasing the variety of tasks, (c) allowing for the self-determination of work pace, (d) increasing responsibility for work quality, (e) increasing discretion over work methods, and (f) allowing for the completion of an entire work unit (Conant and Kilbridge, 1965; Guest, 1957; Hulin and Blood, 1968; Walker, 1950). The literature of the job enlargement movement is replete with studies which conclude that job enlargement in a variety of different forms leads to an array of positive outcomes.[6]

Typical of this literature is a case study reported by Kilbridge (1960). Between 1958 and 1959 the jobs of six centrifugal water pump assemblers were enlarged: each employee who previously performed sequential tasks on a conveyor line began assembling a whole pump, checking the quality of the pump, and stamping it with a personal mark. The time required to assemble a pump dropped from 1.77 minutes to 1.49 minutes; and the annual cost of production dropped from $20,678 to $18,282.

Not all studies of job enlargement, however, yielded such positive results (cf. MacKinney, Wernimont, and Galitz, 1962; Nadler, 1963). Further, Hulin and Blood (1968) concluded that not all employees should be expected to respond positively to job enlargement. These individual differences are discussed in detail in the following chapter.

In summary, job enlargement as a movement in the 1950s and 1960s appeared to yield largely positive results, particularly in regard to job satisfaction. Three issues, however, have created some suspicion concerning job enlargement. First, many of the studies which claimed to report the results of a job enlargement

---

[6]*For example, see Biggane and Stewart (1963); Conant and Kilbridge (1965); Davis and Canter (1956); Davis and Valfer (1965a, b); Davis and Werling (1960); Elliott (1953); Guest (1957); Rice (1953); Trist and Bamforth (1951); Trist, Higgin, Murray, and Pollock (1963); Walker (1950); and Wharton (1954).*

intervention tended to be vague in regard to how the jobs were actually altered and failed to use a conceptual framework or a detailed set of procedures in the enlargement of jobs, leaving unanswered the question, "How does the manager actually go about enlarging a job?" Second, as noted in Chapter 2, several factors (e.g., the employee's aptitudes, skills, and abilities, the employee's role perceptions, and the technology employed) moderate the relationship between effort and performance. These factors have not been systematically considered as constraints on job enlargement or used in developing a conceptual framework for identifying the types of jobs and employees that are prime candidates for job enlargement. Third, many of the studies conducted were methodologically weak and read as if they were published to improve the public image of the firm at which the study was conducted. There is little incentive for a firm to encourage the publication of a study which demonstrates the *failure* of a job enlargement intervention.

JOB ENRICHMENT

In the 1960s, before the impact of job enlargement had been clearly determined, the job enrichment movement came into vogue. The distinction between enlargement and enrichment, however, is somewhat hazy.[7] The advocates of job enrichment (e.g., Herzberg, 1968) argue that the difference between enlargement and enrichment is that enlargement merely makes a job structurally "bigger" (*horizontal job loading*) whereas enrichment provides the opportunity for the employee's psychological growth through vertical job loading. *Vertical loading* refers to adding to a job elements that allow the worker to become more responsible for a total job cycle, from planning and organizing to evaluating results (cf. Rush, 1971).

The vagueness of the enrichment concept was noted and to a degree clarified by Gooding (1970):

Job enrichment is a diffuse, open-ended kind of concept which is more an attitude or strategy than it is a definable

[7]*To confuse the matter more, Herzberg (1974) has interjected the term "orthodox job enrichment."*

entity. In fact, there is no one term for it that is accepted by all the experts. But there are certain elements that appear characteristically wherever job enrichment is going on. Central, of course, is the basic idea of giving the worker more of a say about what he or she is doing, including more responsibility for setting goals, and more responsibility for the excellence of the completed product. It can also mean, in the appropriate kinds of plants, allowing the worker to carry assembly through several stages, sometimes even to completion and preliminary testing, rather than doing just one small operation endlessly (p. 158).

Note the striking similarity between Gooding's description of job enrichment and the definition and elements of job enlargement presented in the preceding section of this chapter. The difference between the two job redesign strategies could be viewed as largely semantic. Nevertheless, because of the popularity of the term, it is worthwhile to examine more closely efforts to apply the enrichment concept and the apparent results of such efforts.

The theoretical basis for job enrichment is commonly recognized as Herzberg's *two-factor theory* (Herzberg, Mausner, and Snyderman, 1959). Essentially, the theory argues that the job content motivators of achievement, recognition, work itself, responsibility, and advancement all contribute to job satisfaction. This satisfaction leads in turn to higher levels of employee performance. Thus, the purpose of job enrichment is to redesign the job to include the motivators listed above. As noted in the previous chapter, the hypothesis that satisfaction causes performance is of questionable validity. In addition, numerous investigators have identified a variety of flaws in the methodology Herzberg employed for the study from which his theory was derived, as well as within the structure of the theory itself.[8]

Even though the theoretical foundation of the job enrichment movement is thus weak, the enrichment literature, like the enlargement literature, is filled with studies which conclude that

[8]*For example, see Dunnette, Campbell, and Hakel (1967); Ewen, Smith, Hulin, and Locke (1966); Graen (1968); Hinrichs and Mischkind (1967); Hinton (1968); House and Wigdor (1967); and King (1970).*

enrichment works.[9] For example, Walton (1972) reported on General Foods' experiences with a plant which opened in Topeka, Kansas, in 1971. The employees of the plant were assigned to teams with a designated team leader; each memeber was required to learn all of the jobs incorporated in the team. Teams were held responsible for correcting customer complaints as well as engaging in the decision-making process in such matters as the level of proficiency and compensation of team members. The results of these and other job enrichment procedures included lower turnover and absenteeism rates, and a rate of productivity 40 percent higher than at other General Foods plants.[10]

Given the similarities between the enlargement and enrichment literatures, the issues previously raised regarding the vitality of enlargement generally also hold true for job enrichment.[11] In other words, the traditional job enrichment literature fails to offer the manager a precise conceptual framework or set of procedures for actually engaging in the process of enrichment, a set of realistic constraints on the potential of enrichment programs, or a sound methodological basis for predicting the impact of enrichment upon labor costs or upon the quantity and quality of productivity. However, recent literature which emerged in the mid-'60s concerning specific task attributes does begin to fill these gaps.

THE TASK ATTRIBUTES LITERATURE

In 1965, Arthur Turner and Paul Lawrence of Harvard University published *Industrial Jobs and the Worker*. Although Turner and Lawrence state that their work was influenced by the

[9]For example, see Doyle (1971); Ford (1969, 1973); Herzberg and Rafalka (1975); Jenkins (1973); Kraft and Williams (1975); Myers (1968, 1970); Paul, Robertson, and Herzberg (1969); Rush (1971); Walton (1972); and Weed (1971).

[10]For a discussion of Walton's 1975 follow-up study on the General Foods experiment, see Chapter 7.

[11]For several interesting discussions of the vitality and future of job enrichment, see Fein (1973, 1974); Hackman (1975); Levitan and Johnston (1973a,b); Parke and Tausky (1975); Plasha (1973); Reif and Luthans (1972); Schappe (1974); Simonds and Orife (1975); Sirota (1973); and Sirota and Wolfson (1972a,b).

FIGURE 3—2   Requisite Task Attributes: Descriptive Scheme

ELEMENTS OF BEHAVIOR

		Activities	Interactions	Mental States
ELEMENTS OF TASK	Prescribed	Variety (Object and Motor)	Required Interaction	Knowledge and Skill
	Discretionary	Autonomy	Optional Interaction (on or off the job)	Responsibility

Adapted from Turner and Lawrence (1965).

research conducted by The Tavistock Institute (e.g., Rice, 1958; Trist and Bamforth, 1951) and The Technology Project of the Institute of Human Relations at Yale, the conceptual framework they employed represents a radical departure from previous job enlargement and job enrichment research. Essentially, Turner and Lawrence hypothesized that a specific set of task attributes directly and indirectly influences the affective and behavioral responses of the employee to the job.

The specific set of task attributes emerged from a classification system (i.e., taxonomy) derived from the earlier works of Homans (1950) and Brown (1960). This taxonomy, presented in Figure 3—2, identified three elements of behavior: *activities*— what people do, in the sense of walking, manipulating tools, etc.; *interactions*—contact between people in which some form of recognizable human exchange occurs; and *mental states*—attitude, feelings, awareness, cognition, etc. Two elements of task are identified: *prescribed*—that part of the task behavior that is programmed or predetermined by the job incumbent's organizationally defined role; and *discretionary*—that behavior which, within prescribed limits, is at the discretion of the individual.

The six task attributes which emerge from this taxonomy are: (1) *variety*—the number of different activities that can be prescribed by various job designs; (2) *autonomy*—the amount of discretion the worker is expected to exercise in carrying out assigned activities; (3) *required interaction*—the amount of necessary interdependence between tasks, particularly that kind of interdependence in which direct face-to-face communication is needed to perform the task properly; (4) *optional interaction*—the amount of voluntary communication feasible given the technology (e.g., machinery layout or noise) employed; (5) *knowledge and skill required*—the degree of mental preparation or learning that can be prescribed as essential in order to perform the job adequately; and (6) *responsibility*—the unprogrammable but necessary level of felt accountability required for task performance. These six task attributes were collectively labeled the *Requisite Task Attributes* (RTA) because they were seen as required by the intrinsic nature of the job.

Turner and Lawrence also identified six *Associated Task Attributes* (ATA): task identity, pay, working conditions, cycle time, level of mechanization, and capital investment. Table 3—1 lists the objective indices Turner and Lawrence used to measure forty-seven jobs on each of the twelve attributes. The jobs were selected from eleven companies representing a broad range of technologies, company sizes, community sizes, and regional settings. Each job was rated in the field by one or more members of the research team. In addition, 470 job occupants completed a job attitude survey which included measures of job satisfaction and perceived task attributes. Attendance data on employees involved in the study was collected from company files.

Turner and Lawrence found that perceived task attribute scores from the job incumbents were positively related to the more objectively measured requisite task attribute scores, and to levels of job satisfaction for the total population studied.[12] Requisite task attribute scores were positively related to attendance for the total population. Optional interaction, learning time, and time span of discretion (an aspect of length of job cycle time) were positively related to job satisfaction.

The systematic investigation of specific task attributes largely lay dormant for six years following this initial study. In 1971, J. Richard Hackman and Edward Lawler III reported the results of another major study of employee reactions to task attri-

[12]*Turner and Lawrence did find significant differences between their town and city subpopulations in regard to the reactions of the employee to the task attributes; such moderators will be discussed in detail in Chapter 5.*

TABLE 3—1   List of Task Attributes and Indices

ACTIVITY

Object Variety
The number of parts, tools, and controls to be manipulated
Motor Variety—average of:
Variety in Prescribed Work Pace
Variety in Physical Location of Work
Variety of Prescribed Physical Operations of Work
Autonomy—average of:
Amount of worker latitude in selection of work methods
Amount of worker latitude in selection of work sequence
Amount of worker latitude in selection of work pace
Amount of worker latitude in accepting or rejecting the quality of
    incoming materials
Amount of worker choice in securing outside services

INTERACTION

Required Interaction—average of:
Number of people required to interact with, at least every two
    hours
Quantity of time spent in required interactions
Optional Interaction On-the-Job—average of:
Number of people available for interaction in working area
Quantity of time available for interaction while working
Optional Interaction Off-the-Job
Amount of time worker is free to choose to leave the work area
    without reprimand

MENTAL STATES

Knowledge and Skill
Amount of time required to learn to perform job proficiently
Responsibility—average of:
Ambiguity of Remedial Action (to correct routine job problems)
Time Span of Discretion—(maximum time before marginal
    substandard work is detected)
Probability of Serious (harmful or costly) Error

ASSOCIATED TASK ATTRIBUTES

Task Identity—average of:
Clarity of Cycle Closure
Visibility of Transformation (performed by the worker)
Visibility (of work transformation) in the Finished Product
Magnitude of (value added by the) Transformation
Pay
Average weekly gross pay without overtime adjusted for U.S. and
    Canadian differential
Working Conditions—average of:
Amount of light and cleanliness in general work area
Table continued.

TABLE 3—1   continued

Amount of fumes, etc.
Temperature
Amount of dirt, grease, oil, in immediate job area
Cycle Time
Length in time of major work cycle
Level of Mechanization
Jobs ranked by the technical sophistication of the machinery used
Capital Investment
Jobs ranked by estimated amount of capital invested per worker

Adapted from Turner and Lawrence (1965).

butes. The attributes investigated by Hackman and Lawler were (1) variety, (2) autonomy, (3) task identity (i.e., the extent to which employees do an entire piece of work and can clearly identify the results of their efforts), (4) feedback, (5) dealing with others, and (6) friendship opportunities. All of these attributes flow directly from the work of Turner and Lawrence, with the possible exception of feedback. Hackman and Lawler define feedback as "the degree to which employees receive information as they are working which reveals how well they are performing on the job" (p. 265).

In addition to other data sources, Hackman and Lawler administered a questionnaire to 208 individuals employed by an eastern telephone company. The employees occupied thirteen different jobs ranging from directory assistance operators to central office repairmen. In general, it was found that the greater the degree of variety, autonomy, task identity, and feedback that employees perceived in their jobs, the more motivated and satisfied they were, the higher their performance, and the better their attendance records. Dealing with others and friendship opportunities were generally found to be unrelated to employee motivation and performance.

In total, these and other studies[13] appear to indicate that

[13]*For example, see Aldag and Brief (1975); Brief and Aldag (1975); Brief, Wallace, and Aldag (1976); Dunham, Aldag, and Brief (1977); Frank and Hackman (1975); Hackman and Oldham (1975); Lawler, Hackman, and Kaufman (1973); Oldham (1976); Oldham, Hackman, and Pearce (1976); Sims and Szilagyi (1976); Sims, Szilagyi, and Keller (1976); Stone (1975, 1976); Stone and Porter (1975); Umstot, Bell, and Mitchell (1976); and Wanous (1974). For reviews of the task attribute literature, see Pierce and Dunham (1976) and Schwab and Cummings (1976).*

an employee's perceptions of four of the task attributes previously mentioned (variety, autonomy, task identity, and feedback) plus one other, task significance, are positively associated with indices of job satisfaction and performance. The additional task attribute, task significance, is defined as "the degree to which the job has a substantial impact on the lives or work of other people—whether in the immediate organization or in the external environment" (Hackman and Oldham, 1975, p. 161).

The relative strength of the associations between these task attributes and job satisfaction and performance suggests a strong task attribute-satisfaction relationship. In short, it appears that task attributes play a more important role in influencing an employee's level of job satisfaction than they do in influencing performance. An explanation for such a finding is offered in the following chapter.

SUMMARY

Out of the long history of work and of attitudes toward it has evolved the modern view that work can serve as a means of fulfilling psychological as well as economic needs. This view is the foundation of the current concern with job design, which may be said to have begun with the scientific management studies of Frederick Taylor and others at the beginning of the twentieth century. While scientific management purportedly offered numerous benefits—increased productivity and lower costs among them—to managers, the costs associated with employee monotony and dissatisfaction were significant.

The job enlargement and job enrichment movements of the 1950s and 1960s attempted to remedy some of the problems resulting from scientific management by expanding, horizontally and vertically, the role of the worker in his job. Both techniques, however, lacked a strong theoretical foundation and the sort of precise conceptual framework necessary to aid managers in actually redesigning jobs. More promising in that respect has been the work of Turner and Lawrence, who in 1965 began a systematic study of specific task attributes. Their work and the work of other researchers since that time has concluded that variety, autonomy, task identity, feedback, and task significance are probably the most significant set of perceived task attributes to consider in the formulation of a job redesign intervention.

REFERENCES

Aldag, R. J., and Brief, A. P. Some correlates of work values. *Journal of Applied Psychology, 60,* 1975, 757–60.

Argyris, C. *Personality and Organization.* New York: Harper & Row, 1957.

Babbage, C. *On the Economy of Machinery and Manufacturers.* London: Charles Knight, 1832.

Bell, D. *Work and Its Discontents: The Cult of Efficiency in America.* Boston: Beacon Press, 1956.

Biggane, J. F., and Stewart, P. A. Job enlargement: A case study. Research series No. 25, State University of Iowa, Iowa City: Bureau of Labor and Management, 1963.

Blauner, R. *Alienation and Freedom.* Chicago: University of Chicago Press, 1964.

Brief, A. P., and Aldag, R. J. Employee reactions to job characteristics: A constructive replication. *Journal of Applied Psychology, 60,* 1975, 182–86.

Brief, A. P., Wallace, M., and Aldag, R. J. Linear vs. non-linear models of the formation of affective responses: The case of job-enlargement. *Decision Sciences, 7,* 1976, 1–9.

Brown, W. *Exploration in Management.* New York: Wiley, 1960.

Conant, E. H., and Kilbridge, M. D. An interdisciplinary analysis of job enlargement: Technology, costs, and behavioral implications. *Industrial and Labor Relations Review, 18,* 1965, 377–95.

Davis, L. E., and Canter, R. R. Job design. *The Journal of Industrial Engineering, 6,* 1955, 3–6, 20.

Davis, L. E., and Canter, R. R. Job design research. *The Journal of Industrial Engineering, 7,* 1956, 275–82.

Davis, L. E., Canter, R. R., and Hoffman, J. Current job design criteria. *The Journal of Industrial Engineering, 6,* 1955, 5–8.

Davis, L. E. Job design and productivity: A new approach. *Personnel, 33,* 1957a, 418–30.

Davis, L. E. Toward a theory of job design. *The Journal of Industrial Engineering, 8,* 1957b, 305–9.

Davis, L. E. The effects of automation on job design. *Industrial Relations, 11,* 1962, 53–71.

Davis, L. E., Cherns, A. B., and Associates. *The Quality of Working Life.* New York: The Free Press, 1975.

Davis, L. E., and Valfer, E. S. Supervisor job design. Proceedings of the Second International Congress on Ergonomics, *Ergonomics, 8,* 1965a, 1.

Davis, L. E., and Valfer, E. S. Intervening responses to changes in supervisors' job designs. *Occupational Psychology, 39,* 1965b, 171–89.

Davis, L. E., and Werling, R. Job design factors. *Occupational Psychology, 34,* 1960, 109–32.

Doyle, F. P. Job enrichment plus OD—A two-pronged approach at Western Union. In *New Perspectives in Job Enrichment,* ed. by J. R. Maher. New York: Van Nostrand-Reinhold, 1971.

Dubin, R. Work in modern society. In *Handbook of Work, Organization, and Society,* ed. by R. Dubin. Chicago: Rand McNally, 1976.

Dunham, R., Aldag, R. J., and Brief, A. P. Dimensionality of task design as measured by the Job Diagnostic Survey. *Academy of Management Journal, 20,* 1977, 209–23.

Dunnette, M. D., Campbell, J. P., and Hakel, M. D. Factors contributing to job satisfaction and dissatisfaction in six occupational groups. *Organizational Behavior and Human Performance, 2,* 1967, 143–74.

Elliot, J. D. Increasing office productivity through job enlargement. In *The Human Side of the Office Manager's Job.* American Management Association, Office Management Series, No. 134, 1953.

Ewen, R. B., Smith, P. C., Hulin, C. L., and Locke, E. A. An empirical test of the Herzberg two-factor theory. *Journal of Applied Psychology, 50,* 1966, 544–50.

Fein, M. The real needs and goals of blue-collar workers. *The Conference Board Record, 10,* 1973, 26–33.

Fein, M. Job enrichment: A reevaluation. *Sloan Management Review, 15,* 1974, 69–88.

Ford, R. N. *Motivation Through Work Itself.* New York: American Management Association, 1969.

Ford, R. N. Job enrichment lessons from AT&T. *Harvard Business Review, 51,* 1973, 96–106.

Frank, L. L., and Hackman, J. R. A failure of job enrichment: The case of the change that wasn't. *Journal of Applied Behavioral Science, 11,* 1975, 413–36.

George, C. S. *The History of Management Thought.* Englewood Cliffs, N.J.: Prentice-Hall, 1968.

Gilbreth, F. B. *Primer of Scientific Management.* New York: Van Nostrand, 1914.

Gillespie, J. J. *Free Expression in Industry: A Social-Psychological Study of Work and Leisure.* London: Pilot Press, 1948.

Golembiewski, R. T. *Men, Management, and Morality: Toward a New Organizational Ethic.* New York: McGraw-Hill, 1965.

Gooding, J. It pays to wake up the blue-collar worker. *Fortune, 82,* 1970, 133–39.

Graen, G. B. Testing traditional and two-factor hypotheses concerning job satisfaction. *Journal of Applied Psychology, 52,* 1968, 366–71.

Guest, R. H. Men and machines: An assembly-line worker looks at his job. *Personnel, 31,* 1955, 496–503.

Guest, R. H. Job enlargement: A revolution in job design. *Personnel Administration, 20,* 1957, 9–16.

Hackman, J. R. On the coming demise of job enrichment. In *Man and Work in Society,* ed. by E. L. Cass and F. G. Zimmer. New York: Van Nostrand-Reinhold, 1975.

Hackman, J. R., and Lawler, E. E., III. Employee reactions to job characteristics. *Journal of Applied Psychology Monograph, 55,* 1971, 259–86.

Hackman, J. R., and Oldham, G. R. Development of the Job Diagnostic Survey. *Journal of Applied Psychology, 60,* 1975, 159–70.

Haimann, T., and Scott, W. G. *Management in the Modern Organization.* 2nd ed. Boston: Houghton Mifflin, 1974.

Heneman, H. G. Work and nonwork: Historical perspectives. In *Work and Nonwork in the Year 2001,* ed. by M. D. Dunnette. Monterey, Calif.: Brooks/Cole, 1973.

Herzberg, F. One more time: How do you motivate employees? *Harvard Business Review, 46,* 1968, 53–62.

Herzberg, F. The wise old Turk. *Harvard Business Review, 52,* 1974, 53–62.

Herzberg, F., Mausner, B., and Snyderman, B. *The Motivation to Work.* New York: Wiley, 1959.

Herzberg, F., and Rafalka, E. Efficiency in the military: Cutting costs with orthodox job enrichment. *Personnel, 52,* 1975, 38–48.

Hinrichs, J. R. Psychology of men at work. In *Annual Review of Psychology,* Vol. 21, ed. by P. Mussen and M. Rosenzweig. Palo Alto, Calif.: Annual Review, Inc., 1970.

Hinrichs, J. R., and Mischkind, L. A. Empirical and theoretical limitations of the two-factor hypothesis of job satisfaction. *Journal of Applied Psychology, 51,* 1967, 191–200.

Hinton, B. L. An empirical investigation of the Herzberg methodology and two-factor theory. *Organizational Behavior and Human Performance, 3,* 1968, 286–309.

Homans, G. *The Human Group.* New York: Harcourt Brace Jovanovich, 1950.

House, R. J., and Wigdor, L. Herzberg's dual-factor theory of job satisfaction and motivation: A review of the evidence and a criticism. *Personnel Psychology, 20,* 1967, 369–89.

Hulin, C. L., and Blood, M. R. Job enlargement, individual differences, and worker responses. *Psychological Bulletin, 69,* 1968, 41–55.

Jasinski, F. J. Technological delimitation of reciprocal relationships: A study of interaction patterns in industry. *Human Organization, 15,* 1956, 24–28.

Jenkins, D. *Job Power: Blue and White Collar Democracy.* Garden City, N.Y.: Doubleday, 1973.

Kennedy, E. M. *Worker Alienation,* 1972. (Subcommittee on Employment, Manpower, and Poverty of the United States Senate). Washington, D.C.: U.S. Government Printing Office, 1972.

Kilbridge, M. D. Reduced costs through job enrichment: A case. *The Journal of Business, 33,* 1960, 357–62.

King, N. A clarification and evaluation of the two-factor theory of job satisfaction. *Psychological Bulletin, 74,* 1970, 18–31.

Kornhauser, A. W. *Mental Health of the Industrial Worker: A Detroit Study.* New York: Wiley, 1965.

Kraft, W. P., and Williams, K. L. Job redesign improves productivity. *Personnel Journal, 54,* 1975, 393–97.

Lawler, E. E., III. *Motivation in Work Organizations.* Monterey, Calif.: Brooks/Cole, 1973.

Lawler, E. E., III, Hackman, J. R., and Kaufman, S. Effects of job redesign: A field experiment. *Journal of Applied Social Psychology, 3,* 1973, 49–62.

Levitan, S. A., and Johnston, W. B. *Work Is Here to Stay, Alas.* Salt Lake City: Olympus, 1973a.

Levitan, S. A., and Johnston, W. B. Job redesign, reform, enrichment—exploring the limitations. *Monthly Labor Review, 96,* 1973b, 35–41.

Likert, R. *New Patterns of Management.* New York: McGraw-Hill, 1961.

Macy, B. A., and Mirvis, P. H. A methodology for assessment of quality of work life and organizational effectiveness in behavioral-economic terms. *Administrative Science Quarterly, 21,* 1976, 212-26.

MacKinney, A. C., Wernimont, P. F., and Galitz, W. O. Has specialization reduced job satisfaction? *Personnel, 39,* 1962, 8-17.

McFarland, D. E. *Management: Principles and Practices.* 4th ed. New York: Macmillan, 1974.

McGregor, D. M. An uneasy look at performance appraisal. *Harvard Business Review, 35,* 1957, 89-94.

Mills, C. W. *White Collar.* New York: Oxford University Press, 1956.

Munsterberg, H. *Psychology and Industrial Efficiency.* Boston: Houghton Mifflin, 1913.

Myers, M. S. Every employee a manager. *California Management Review, 10,* 1968, 9-20.

Myers, M. S. *Every Employee a Manager: More Meaningful Work Through Job Enrichment.* New York: McGraw-Hill, 1970.

Nadler, G. *Work Design.* Homewood, Ill.: Irwin, 1963.

Oldham, G. R. Job characteristics and internal motivation: The moderating effect of interpersonal and individual variables. *Human Relations, 29,* 1976, 559-69.

Oldham, G. R., Hackman, J. R., and Pearce, J. L. Conditions under which employees respond positively to enriched work. *Journal of Applied Psychology, 61,* 1976, 395-403.

Parke, E. L., and Tausky, C. The mythology of job enrichment: Self actualization revisited. *Personnel, 52,* 1975, 12-21.

Parker, S. R., and Smith, M. A. Work and leisure. In *Handbook of Work, Organization, and Society,* ed. by R. Dubin. Chicago: Rand McNally, 1976.

Paul, W. J., Jr., Robertson, K. B., and Herzberg, F. Job enrichment pays off. *Harvard Business Review, 47,* 1969, 61-78.

Pierce, J. L., and Dunham, R. B. Task design: A literature review. *The Academy of Management Review, 1,* 1976, 83-97.

Plasha, F. Job enrichment: Evangelist or carpetbagger of the 70's? *Personnel Administrator, 43,* 1973, 48-51.

Reif, W. E., and Luthans, F. Does job enrichment really pay off? *California Management Review, 15,* 1972, 30-37.

Rice, A. K. Productivity and social organization in an Indian weaving shed. *Human Relations, 6,* 1953, 297–329.

Rice, A. K. *Productivity and Social Organization: The Ahnedabad Experiment.* London: Tavistock, 1958.

Rush, H. M. F. *Job Design for Motivation.* New York: The Conference Board, 1971.

Schappe, R. H. Twenty-two arguments against job enrichment. *Personnel Journal, 53,* 1974, 116–23.

Schwab, D. P., and Cummings, L. L. A theoretical analysis of the impact of task scope on employee performance. *The Academy of Management Review, 1,* 1976, 23–35.

Shapiro, H. J., and Wahba, M. A. Frederick W. Taylor: 62 years later. *Personnel Journal, 53,* 1974, 574–78.

Sheppard, H. L., and Herrick, N. *Where Have All the Robots Gone?* New York: The Free Press, 1972.

Simonds, R. H., and Orife, J. N. Worker behavior versus enrichment theory. *Administrative Science Quarterly, 20,* 1975, 606–12.

Sims, H. P., Jr., and Szilagyi, A. D. Job characteristic relationships: Individual and structural moderators. *Organizational Behavior and Human Performance, 17,* 1976, 211–30.

Sims, H. P., Jr., Szilagyi, A. D., and Keller, R. T. The measurement of job characteristics. *Academy of Management Journal, 19,* 1976, 195–212.

Sirota, D. Production and service personnel and job enrichment. *Work Study, 22,* 1973, 9–15.

Sirota, D., and Wolfson, A. D. Job enrichment: What are the obstacles? *Personnel, 49,* 1972a, 8–17.

Sirota, D., and Wolfson, A. D. Job enrichment: Surmounting the obstacles. *Personnel, 49,* 1972b, 8–19.

Stone, E. F. Job scope, job satisfaction and the Protestant Ethic: A study of enlisted men in the U.S. Navy. *Journal of Vocational Behavior, 7,* 1975, 215–24.

Stone, E. F. The moderating effect of work-related values on the job scope–job satisfaction relationship. *Organizational Behavior and Human Performance, 15,* 1976, 147–67.

Stone, E. F., and Porter, L. W. Job characteristics and job attitudes: A multivariate study. *Journal of Applied Psychology, 60,* 1975, 57–64.

Taylor, F. W. *Shop Management.* New York: Harper, 1903.

Taylor, F. W. *The Principles of Scientific Management.* New York: Harper, 1911.

Taylor, F. W. *Scientific Management.* New York: Harper & Row, 1947.

Tilgher, A. *Work: What It Has Meant to Man Through the Ages.* London: Harrap, 1931.

Trist, E. L., and Bamforth, K. W. Some social and psychological consequences of the longwall method of coal-getting. *Human Relations, 4,* 1951, 3-38.

Trist, E. L., Higgin, G. W., Murray, H., and Pollock, A. B. *Organizational Choice.* London: Tavistock, 1963.

Turner, A. N. A researcher views adjustment to automation. *Advanced Management, 21,* 1956, 21-25.

Turner, A. N., and Lawrence, P. R. *Industrial Jobs and the Worker.* Cambridge: Harvard University, Graduate School of Business Administration, 1965.

Turner, A. N., and Miclette, A. L. Sources of satisfaction in repetitive work. *Occupational Psychology, 36,* 1962, 215-31.

Umstot, D. D., Bell, C. H., and Mitchell, T. R. Effects of job enrichment and task goals on satisfaction and productivity: Implications for job design. *Journal of Applied Psychology, 61,* 1976, 379-94.

Walker, C. R. The problem of the repetitive job. *Harvard Business Review, 28,* 1950, 54-58.

Walker, C. R. Work methods, working conditions and morale. In *Industrial Conflict,* ed. by A. Kornhauser, R. Dubin, and A. M. Ross. New York: McGraw-Hill, 1954.

Walker, C. R. *Modern Technology and Civilization.* New York: McGraw-Hill, 1962.

Walker, C. R., and Guest, R. H. *The Man on the Assembly Line.* Cambridge: Harvard University Press, 1952.

Walker, C. R., Guest, R. H., and Turner, A. N. *The Foreman on the Assembly Line.* Cambridge: Harvard University Press, 1956.

Walton, R. E. How to counter alienation in the plant. *Harvard Business Review, 50,* 1972, 70-81.

Walton, R. E. Quality of working life: What is it? *Sloan Management Review, 15,* 1973, 11-21.

Wanous, J. P. Individual differences and reactions to job characteristics. *Journal of Applied Psychology, 59,* 1974, 616-22.

Weed, E. D. Job enrichment "cleans up" at Texas Instruments. In *New Perspectives in Job Enrichment,* ed. by J. R. Maher. New York: Van Nostrand-Reinhold, 1971.

Wharton, D. Removing monotony from factory jobs. *American Mercury,* 1954, 91–95.

Whyte, W. F. *Money and Motivation.* New York: Harper & Row, 1955.

Work in America. Report of Special Task Force to Secretary of Health, Education, and Welfare. Washington, D.C.: U.S. Government Printing Office, 1972.

Job Design and   4
Employee Motivation:
A Synthesis

As noted in the previous chapter, Turner and Lawrence attempted to measure both the objective attributes of a job and the job incumbent's perceptions of those attributes. Other researchers (e.g., Brief, Aldag, and Jacox, in press; Hackman and Lawler, 1971; Pierce and Dunham, 1976; Schwab and Cummings, 1976) have noted the distinction between and importance of measuring both the *objective* set of activities which comprise the job and the job incumbent's *perceptions* of those activities in terms of the identified task attributes. Put simply, employees often react to their perceptions of the job's content, which do not necessarily coincide with the actual content of the job. Furthermore, the manager cannot directly change the job incumbent's perceptions and must instead attempt to alter the objective content of the job in order to influence employee perceptions.[1] Figure 4—1 depicts this relationship between the actual task ac-

[1]*Failures of researchers in their attempts to manipulate employee perceptions of the task attributes (e.g., Frank and Hackman, 1975; Lawler, Hackman, and Kaufman, 1973) highlight the practical need for considering both the objective and perceptual characteristics of the job.*

tivities which comprise the job and the employee's perceptions of the task attributes.

The model in Figure 4—1 goes on to specify one way of viewing the determinants of an employee's reaction to the content of a job.[2] First, it can be seen that two other sets of employee perceptions, valences and instrumentalities of task attributes, are salient factors to be considered. It should be recalled that these two concepts were introduced in Chapter 2 when the expectancy model of motivation was discussed. If the employee perceives the task attributes to be positively valent (i.e., the employee anticipates an increase in satisfaction by experiencing the attributes), then the attributes will play a positive role in increasing motivation.

Further, the valence of each attribute is weighted by the perceived likelihood that performance will in fact lead to experiencing the attribute (i.e., the instrumentality of the attribute). Thus, if the employee perceives a strong positive association between performance and the attribute, motivation will be even further enhanced.

Assuming the employee perceives the task attributes to be present in a job and positively valent, the third component of the model can be considered. Here the employee associates job behaviors with the task attributes. As discussed in Chapter 2, such associations yield a state of intrinsic motivations in which the employee feels freely vested in the job.

This state of intrinsic motivation will influence the employee's reactions to the job in at least one or two ways. First, if the employee perceives the task attributes as being present in the job and positively valent, the employee will react positively towards the job in terms of high satisfaction and a strong attachment to and involvement in the job. Behaviorally, such an affective state should translate into reduced tardiness, absenteeism, and turnover. Furthermore, as previously noted, this state of intrinsic motivation may be directly associated with task persistence.

Second, if the employee perceives the task attributes as being present in the job, positively valent, and contingent upon

[2]Some of the ideas presented in the model are drawn in part from the works of Lawler (1969); Salancik and Pfeffer (1976); Staw (1976); Steers and Mowday (1976); and Umstot, Bell, and Mitchell (1976).

FIGURE 4—1   A Model of Employee Reactions to Their Jobs

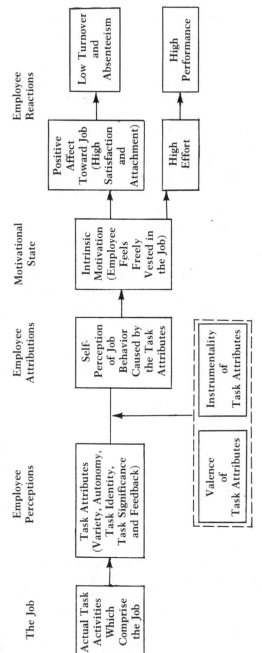

performance, the employee's reactions will take the form of increased effort—effort which will, within certain constraints previously discussed, translate into increased performance. Performance is defined in terms of quantity or quality of *productivity* dependent upon the performance-task attribute contingencies and the nature of the employee's performance goals.

The above employee reaction model in large part incorporates Chapter 2's discussion of intrinsic motivation. The salient theme is that the task attributes (variety, autonomy, task identity, task significance, and feedback) perceived in an employee's job should lead to increased satisfaction if the attributes are positively valent to the employee. If the attributes are positively valent *and* felt to be contingent upon performance, the attributes should also yield increased performance levels.

Finally, although the model does not explicitly address the goal-setting process, it should be noted that a large number of studies indicate that the specification and acceptance of performance goals have a strong influence on employee performance.[3] In essence, it has been shown that setting specific rather than generalized (e.g., "Do your best") or no goals, and difficult rather than easy goals leads to higher levels of performance. Thus it behooves the manager to set specific, hard goals for his subordinate, regardless of whether or not that manager is concerned with job redesign or any other motivational strategy.

Having now introduced a model depicting the reactions of employees to the content of their jobs, we must turn to the question of how one can make practical use of that model in an organization.

HOW TO REDESIGN JOBS

The first step to consider when contemplating a job redesign intervention is an assessment of need. If for a given set of jobs turnover and absenteeism are judged to be exceedingly costly, or performance, in terms of the quantity or quality of productivity, appears to be below par, then the manager should

[3]For reviews of this literature, see Latham and Yukl (1975); Locke (1968); Locke, Cartledge, and Knerr (1970); and Locke, Cartledge, and Koeppel (1968).

engage in a search process to identify possible intervention strategies. It generally appears worthwhile to consider a job redesign program as a tentative solution when:

1. The target jobs can be characterized as simplified, demanding a low skill level, and consisting of short-cycle completion sequences: in other words, jobs which incumbents perceive as monotonous.

2. Extrinsic outcomes are available at sufficiently high levels so as not to serve as a major source of irritation to job incumbents. For example, wages paid should be equivalent to those paid people performing similar activities both within the local labor market and within the employing organization.[4]

3. The current technology being employed does not in the short term prohibit the redesign of jobs due to the high cost of new capital investment that might be required. This condition really addresses a two-fold question. First, in an engineering sense, is it feasible to alter the methods and procedures of production, given the constraints imposed by the current set of production facilities and techniques? Second, is it economically feasible to consider replacement of the current set of production facilities and techniques?

4. The current and potential incumbents of the target jobs are ready for a job redesign intervention.[5] Readiness essentially consists of two components: the pool of incumbents perceives the task attributes of variety, autonomy, task identity, etc., as positively valent and possesses (or is capable of possessing through retraining) the set of aptitudes, skills, and abilities which might be required by a job redesign intervention.

[4]*Probably the best way of assessing a job incumbent's reactions to the degree of monotony in a job and the levels of available extrinsic outcomes is to have the incumbent complete a standard job satisfaction instrument. For example, The Job Descriptive Index (JDI) developed by Smith, Kendall, and Hulin (1969) measures satisfaction with the work itself, pay, promotional opportunities, supervision, and co-workers. If the incumbent scores relatively high on the other extrinsic facets, then one should go on to consider items (3) and (4) discussed above.*
[5]*Procedures for measuring psychological readiness for job redesign interventions are discussed in the next chapter.*

If it is determined that all these criteria are met, then there is probably sufficient evidence to assume that a job redesign intervention may lead to increased job satisfaction and increased job effort. As is the case with assessing the need for some intervention, the above determination should be made collectively by management, labor, and any third parties whose expertise may be required. Further, the processes of need assessment and of determining the initial feasibility of a job redesign intervention should be thoughtful and thorough, rather than emotionally charged and haphazard.[6]

Once the decision has been made to further explore job redesign as a solution alternative, an organizational unit should be designated responsible for further exploring the possibilities and for issuing a set of specific recommendations in a timely fashion. This unit should probably take the form of a *job redesign task force* which would be composed of representatives of management and labor as well as ad hoc technical specialists as needed. The representatives from management and labor should be drawn from the positions depicted in Figure 4—2. In essence, all parties who may have the structure of their job altered should be represented.

The first activity of the task force should be to obtain hard data regarding the actual task activities which comprise the target jobs, the jobs which are sequentially linked to the target jobs, and jobs of those supervisors which may be affected. By *sequentially linked,* we mean those jobs which provide materials and support services which are required by the incumbents of the target jobs in order to perform effectively (e.g., unfinished products and maintenance) and those which receive materials and support services from the incumbents of the target jobs. Job redesign does not occur in isolation: activities typically are drawn from the jobs which surround the target jobs.

In many organizations, the lists of job activities are readily available from the job analyses which have previously been per-

_____

[6]*A job redesign intervention can be viewed as a major organizational change or as an organizational development strategy. Thus, many of the suggestions offered in this section are drawn from the organization change and organizational development literatures. For reviews of these literatures, see Alderfer (1976); Argyris (1971); Beckhard (1969); Beer (1976); Bennis (1966, 1969); Schein (1969); and Schein and Bennis (1965).*

FIGURE 4—2 Parties to Be Represented on the Job Redesign Task Force

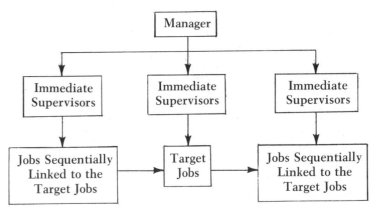

formed. A job analysis is a set of observational procedures which yield a description of what a job incumbent does, as well as how and why the incumbent does it. Such job-related information serves as a basic ingredient in the personnel practices of many organizations. If, however, the required list of activities is not available, the task force must proceed to acquire the necessary information in order to know precisely the activities which comprise the jobs under review. One method of conducting a job analysis is to use a *job inventory*, a structured questionnaire consisting of a list of tasks relevant to jobs within some occupational area. The respondent indicates the significance of each task to the job in terms of how much time is spent on the task, how important the task is to the position, how much a part of the job the task is, or how frequently the task is performed (cf., McCormick, 1976). The procedures for developing and administering job inventories are well known and readily available.[7] Figure 4—3 presents a portion of a job inventory for the outside wire and antenna systems career field of the Air Force.

Once the content of the relevant set of jobs has been iden-

[7]For discussions of job analysis techniques, see McCormick (1976); McCormick, Jeanneret, and Mecham (1972); Prien and Ronan (1971); and Tiffin and McCormick (1965). The question of job analysis will be examined in greater detail in the following section of this chapter.

FIGURE 4—3 A Portion of a Job Inventory for the Outside Wire and Antenna Systems Career Field of the Air Force

Listed below is a duty and the tasks which it includes. Check all tasks which you perform. Add any tasks you do which are not listed. Then rate the tasks you have checked.

H. INSTALLING AND REMOVING AERIAL CABLE SYSTEMS	CHECK IF DONE	TIME SPENT 1. Very much below average 2. Below average 3. Slightly below average 4. About average 5. Slightly above average 6. Above average 7. Very much above average	IMPORTANCE 1. Extremely unimportant 2. Very unimportant 3. Unimportant 4. About medium importance 5. Important 6. Very important 7. Extremely important
1. Attach suspension strand to pole			
2. Change and splice lasher wire			
3. Deliver materials to lineman with snatch block and handline			
4. Drill through-bolt holes and secure suspension clamps on poles			
5. Install cable pressurization systems			
6. Install distribution terminals			
7. Install pulling-in line through cable rings			
8. Load and unload cable reels			
9. Load lashing machine with lashing wire			

From McCormick (1976) who originally adapted from Morsh and Archer (1967)

tified, the task force should proceed to explore the relationships between the activities identified through the job analysis and the perceived presence of the salient task attributes (variety, autonomy, task identity, etc.). In other words, the task force must attempt to answer the very difficult question of what actual job activities would lead a job incumbent to perceive the presence of each of the six task attributes in a job. Three procedures should be used to identify job activity–task attribute relationships. First, for the target jobs and those jobs surrounding them, the relationships between responses to an instrument like the job inventory should be correlated to the responses to one of several instruments designed to gauge an employee's perceptions of the degree to which the task attributes are present in the job.[8]

Second, members of the task force should interview some of the occupants of the relevant set of jobs. The purpose of such interviews is to supplement with specific and meaningful examples the previous analysis. The employees' perceptions of the task attributes and the activities which they feel to be associated with those perceptions should be informally explored. For example, one may want to ask a job incumbent, "How much discretion (i.e., autonomy) do you exercise over how and when you get the various parts of your job done? Can you give some specific examples of activities over which you exercise a great deal of discretion?" For future use members would also want to ask, "Do you have any specific suggestions for increasing the amount of autonomy you have in your job?" Besides providing a rich source of data, these interviews increase the employees' feelings of being an integral part of the redesign process.

Finally, the task force members should discuss collectively their feelings about job activity–task attribute relationships. The caveats for such discussions should be openness and candor. The purpose of these discussions is to allow all task force members to examine publicly their own perceptions, and to educate the other members about the content of their jobs and the presence of the salient task attributes.

The task force should then begin to formulate a specific redesign intervention. Rather than attempting to tackle all six

[8]*Some of the instruments designed to gauge employee perceptions of the task attributes include the Yale Job Inventory (Hackman and Lawler, 1971); the Job Diagnostic Survey (Hackman and Oldham, 1975); and the Job Characteristic Inventory (Sims, Szilagyi, and Keller, 1976).*

task attributes at once, the task force will probably be better off to focus, as far as is feasible, upon one attribute at a time. Again, the purpose of the redesign is to alter the activities which comprise the target jobs in such a way as to increase the degree to which the employee perceives each task attribute to be present in the job.

Assume that the task force has decided that the job incumbents are particularly concerned with increased autonomy. The first redesign procedure would therefore be to identify those activities which, when added to the job, would most likely increase perceptions of autonomy.

The basis for such an identification would be the data collected regarding job activity-task attribute relationships. In addition, the members of the task force should draw upon their own creativity in identifying other activities which may lead to increased autonomy. In essence, the task force will examine those activities currently incorporated in the jobs which surround the target jobs and those activities centered elsewhere in the organization which can realistically be added to the target jobs. In identifying such activities, the task force should ensure that a) it is technologically feasible to locate the activity in the target jobs; b) the incumbents of the target jobs wish to perform the particular activity and are able or willing to be trained to do so; c) the previous performers of the activity are willing to give it up or have it replaced; and d) the likelihood of making the activity contingent upon some performance level, so that both the effect and the effort of the incumbents may be enhanced, is high. Such issues should be resolved by the task force collectively and in discussions with the parties whose jobs will be affected. As far as is possible, a consensus to proceed with the particular intervention should be reached.

For example, one of the task force members, as well as some of the incumbents of the target jobs, might suggest that one way to increase autonomy would be to allow the incumbents, within certain limits (e.g., the workday must consist of eight hours), to determine when they would start and end their workday.[9] The task force might then determine that a) the flexible

[9]For reviews of the literature of the impact of "Flexitime," see Allenspach (1972); Baum and Young (1973); Evans (1973); Golembiewski, Hilles, and Kagno (1974); Golembiewski, Yeager, and Hilles (1975); Holly, Armenakis, and Field (1976); and Partridge (1973).

work scheduling would not disrupt the flow of production; b) the job incumbents were in general agreement that the flexible work scheduling was desirable and that they were willing to learn how to schedule and record their time on the job; c) the personnel department which had been vested with scheduling working hours and the supervisors who had been charged with monitoring working hours were willing to go along with the idea; and d) only those incumbents who perform at a predetermined level from month to month would have the opportunity to schedule their work hours.

Following the formalization of an intervention, the task force should select, with their concurrence, a number of the job incumbents to serve as subjects in a study designed to evaluate the impact of the intervention.[10] The intervention at this stage should be viewed as a good idea worthy of rigorous evaluation, not as a sure cure-all. The criteria to be employed in the evaluations should include measures of satisfaction and performance as well as cost-benefit data to ensure that the intervention is economically feasible.[11] Finally, steps must be taken if needed to begin to redesign the physical aspects of the work environment and to train the subjects in the performance of their new activities.

Following completion of the evaluation study, assuming the results were positive, the task force should take steps to diffuse the intervention throughout all of the incumbents of the target jobs. The reconstruction of the work environment and the retraining of personnel should now proceed if necessary.

Several additional points about the above process should be noted. First, as is apparent, the job redesign process takes time. One should not expect to accomplish a major job redesign intervention in the period of a few weeks. Several sets of target jobs and several task attributes within a given target job, however, can be redesigned simultaneously. Finally, as noted earlier, the activities added to the target jobs are taken from other positions in the organization. Thus, the logical conclusion of a job redesign intervention is a change in several jobs throughout the

[10]For materials regarding the design of such evaluative studies, see Caro (1971); Cook and Campbell (1976); Guttentag and Struening (1976); and Suchman (1967).
[11]For discussions of such cost-benefit type of analyses, see Macy and Mirvis (1976); Mirvis and Lawler (1977); Mirvis and Macy (1976); and Rhode and Lawler (1973).

organization, and thus a change in the structure of the organiza-
tion—the topic of Chapter 6.

OBJECTIVE JOB CHARACTERISTICS

The discussion of the job redesign process just presented
stressed the need to assess objective job characteristics. This
section looks more closely at some techniques which are useful
for that purpose, including motion study, time study, and job
analysis. To some extent, it may seem strange to include a discus-
sion of such topics as time and motion study in a book which has
stressed the fact that it is often desirable to let employees do the
planning and control of their work. However, it can be argued
that it is desirable to do any job efficiently, no matter how en-
riched it is. As such, the techniques outlined in this section
should be viewed as useful complements to enrichment attempts
or other redesign efforts. Further, if we are to get an adequate
objective picture of the job as it currently exists—as we should
prior to undertaking any redesign projects—such techniques can
be very helpful.

Motion study

One important element of job design is the determination
of the most efficient method to perform the job, sometimes called
motion study.[12] The purposes of motion study are to find ways to
do the job which minimize such variables as effort, cost, and
difficulty, while optimally using manpower, machinery, and
materials. Motion study tools fall into three categories, which
differ in their degree of detail: process analysis, activity analysis,
and operation analysis.

Process analysis • Process analysis takes a broad view of
work design, evaluating the flow of work. A *flow process chart* is
used to provide an overall picture of the steps from the beginning

[12]*The discussion of motion and time study are drawn largely from Laufer
(1975).*

TABLE 4—1   Process Analysis Symbols

Symbol	Symbol Name	Description
O	Operation	A change in an item, such as in size or shape, occurs.
⇨	Transportation	An item or individual moves from one workplace to another.
D	Delay	An item or individual must wait.
△	Storage	A controlled storage condition exists in which an order is needed to take the item out of storage and move it to the next scheduled activity.
☐	Inspection	An item is compared to some standard.

to the end of the job. A man-type process chart tracks the activities of an individual, while a material process chart considers processes involving materials. The symbols most commonly used in such charts, presented in Table 4—1, are modifications of the four originally developed by Frank and Lillian Gilbreth.

Activity analysis • Activity analysis is one way to consider the job in more detail. An *activity chart* plots each operation in a process against a time scale. For example, activity analysis might be used to detail and attach times to the movements of a dental assistant preparing dental cement. *Multiactivity charts* depict details of tasks performed by an individual in situations where other individuals or machines affect the time required to complete the task. One such chart is the *man-machine chart* which, by considering times taken by the worker and other workers or machines, can be used to determine whether there is idle time which can be reduced or eliminated.

Operation analysis • Operation analysis is used to examine a method in minute detail. In particular, the motions of each hand are analyzed. One form of operation analysis, termed *micromotion analysis,* uses motion pictures to record actions and to allow their subsequent timing. Seventeen fundamental hand motions, named *therbligs* (from *Gilbreth,* roughly spelled backwards) are used to describe the work done by each hand. Some

TABLE 4—2   Selected Therbligs

Therblig Name	Therblig Symbol	Description
Search	SH	Trying to find item by using hands or eyes
Assemble	A	Putting items together
Inspect	I	Examination of an item to determine quality
Hold	H	Maintaining an item in a fixed position
Position	P	Lining up, locating, or orienting an item

therbligs and their symbols and descriptions are presented in Table 4—2. Clearly, the cost and effort of such a procedure would generally be justified only in the case of repetitive operations.

Time study

Time study and motion study are closely interrelated. Once a method is selected to perform an operation, time study can be used to find the *standard time* for the operation; that is, the time needed by a qualified operator to perform the operation while working at a normal pace. Such standard times can be used in scheduling, setting wage incentives, manpower planning, and formulating budgets. Further, comparison of actual and planned times is useful for control purposes.[13]

Job analysis

Job analysis involves the collection of information concerning the job. Job analysis programs may differ in terms of types of information obtained, the form in which the information is obtained, the method of analysis used, and the individual or device used to collect the information. For example, information might be collected concerning work activities, job content, work

[13]*Time study is one technique of work measurement. For a discussion of other work measurement techniques, including elemental standard data systems, motion-time data systems, and work sampling, see Laufer (1975).*

performance, personnel requirements, and so on.[14] The form of information could be qualitative (such as verbal statements) or quantitative (such as size of the work group). Data might be collected by means of structured questionnaires, observation, interviews, or any of a number of other methods. The information might be collected by a job analyst, the worker, the worker's supervisor, cameras, physiological recording devices, and so on.

Unfortunately, the history of job analysis has been somewhat disappointing, characterized by semantic confusion, high degrees of subjectivity, and a general lack of rigorous, systematic procedures. However, there have been some attempts to systematically examine jobs. For example, time and motion studies provide useful information concerning the job, though the range of job-related information they yield is very limited. As noted earlier, some more inclusive approaches to job analysis involving the use of structured questionnaires have recently been developed.

One currently popular way to analyze the job is by use of the *Position Analysis Questionnaire* (PAQ).[15] In developing the PAQ, McCormick and his associates hypothesized that there is an underlying structure or order to the domain of human work. In particular, this structure may be reflected in the way that specific *units* of job-related variables tend to be organized across jobs. It was felt that once such elemental "building blocks" were identified, it would be possible to see how they fit together to describe various jobs. By comparing job-dimension scores for different jobs, job profiles could be developed. This is analogous to the approach taken in the physical sciences, where it is recognized that while things may be very different in many ways, they are composed of the same basic units.

In deciding how to approach the isolation of those building blocks, McCormick's earlier (1959) distinction between job-oriented and worker-oriented job elements was considered. *Job-oriented elements* are descriptions of job content associated with the technological aspects of jobs and generally reflect what is achieved by the worker. *Worker-oriented elements* characterize the human behaviors involved. Since job-oriented elements are likely

[14]For a thorough discussion of job analysis, see McCormick (1976).
[15]For a more thorough discussion of the PAQ, see McCormick, Jeanneret, and Mecham (1972) and McCormick (1976). The PAQ can be obtained from the University Book Store, West Lafayette, Indiana 47906.

TABLE 4—3   PAQ Divisions, Subdivisions, and Specific Examples

Information Input (35)
Sources of job information (20): Use of written materials
Discrimination and perceptual activities (15): Estimating speed of
  moving objects

Mediation Processes (14)
Decision making and reasoning (2): Reasoning in problem solving
Information processing (6): Encoding, decoding
Use of stored information (6): Using mathematics

Work Output (50)
Use of physical devices (29): Use of keyboard devices
Integrative manual activities (8): Handling objects, materials
General body activities (7): Climbing
Manipulation, coordination activities (6): Hand-arm manipulation

Interpersonal Activities (36)
Communications (10): Instructing
Interpersonal relationships (3): Serving/catering
Personal contact (15): Personal contact with public customers
Supervision and coordination (8): Level of supervision received

Work Situation and Job Context (18)
Physical working conditions (12): Low temperature
Psychological and sociological aspects (6): Civic obligations

Miscellaneous Aspects (36)
Work schedule, method of pay, and apparel (21): Irregular hours
Job demands (12): Specified (controlled) work pace
Responsibility (3): Responsibility for safety of others

From McCormick et al. (1972). Numbers of items are in parentheses.

to differ substantially across jobs, the approach taken in de-
veloping the PAQ relied instead upon the determination of
worker-oriented elements. Further, those worker-oriented ele-
ments could be viewed as relating to information input, media-
tion processes, output, and the behavioral "adjustment" required
of individuals to features of the job environment.

The PAQ consists of 189 worker-oriented job elements. A
listing of the major divisions and subdivisions of the PAQ and the
number of items included in each is presented in Table 4—3. A
variety of rules are used for the various job elements (for exam-
ple, importance, extent of use, and so on). Statistical analyses of
the PAQ elements within each of the major divisions resulted in

TABLE 4—4   Dimensions of Information Inputs

Visual input from devices/materials
Perceptual interpretation
Information from people
Visual input from distal sources
Evaluation of information from physical sources
Environmental awareness
Awareness of body movement/posture

From McCormick et al. (1972).

the discovery of specific job dimensions,[16] such as the dimensions of information input presented in Table 4—4.

Studies which have considered the statistical characteristics of the PAQ have yielded favorable results. The PAQ has been used successfully to help in determining job values for pay purposes, in establishing aptitude requirements for jobs, and in a number of other situations. In the context of job design, the PAQ promises to be a useful tool for the assessment of objective task characteristics, which is crucial in the overall process of job design.

SUMMARY

The primary purpose of this chapter has been to synthesize the job design literature into a practical working plan for managers and organizations who wish to undertake a job redesign intervention. The model of employee reactions to a job, which we presented as a foundation for this plan, considers the actual activities which comprise the job, the perceptions and attributions of the employee, the employee's motivational state, and the affective and behavioral reactions of the employee. As far as possible, we have also tried to provide the tools necessary to measure all these variables. The intervention strategy itself is summarized for the reader in Figure 4—4.

[16]*A number of other procedures were also used. For example, psychologists were asked to rate how much of various attributes (such as intelligence, perceptual speed, empathy, stage presence, and mechanical ability) were required for each element. By getting attribute scores for each element and then statistically analyzing those scores, it was possible to obtain dimensions based on attribute profiles.*

FIGURE 4—4   A Proposed Job Redesign Strategy

Identification of a
Need for a
Behavioral Intervention

↓

Determination of the
Initial Feasibility
of Job Redesign

↓

Creation of a
Labor-Management Job
Redesign Task Force

↓

Identification of
Actual Activities
Comprising the Job

↓

Identification of
Job Activities–
Task Attribute Linkages

↓

Specification of
Specific Job Redesign
Intervention

↓

Evaluation of
Proposed
Intervention

↓

Diffusion of
Intervention

REFERENCES

Alderfer, C. P. Change processes in organizations. In *Handbook of Industrial and Organizational Psychology*, ed. by M. D. Dunnette. Chicago: Rand McNally, 1976.

Allenspach, H. Flexible working time: Its development and application in Switzerland. *Occupational Psychology, 46*, 1972, 209–15.

Argyris, C. *Management and Organizational Development: The Path from X_a to X_b*. New York: McGraw-Hill, 1971.

Baum, S. J., and Young, W. M. *A Practical Guide to Flexible Working Hours*. Park Ridge, N.J.: Noyes Data Corporation, 1973.

Beckhard, R. *Organization Development: Strategies and Models*. Reading, Mass.: Addison-Wesley, 1969.

Beer, M. The technology of organizational development. In *Handbook of Industrial and Organizational Psychology*, ed. by M. D. Dunnette. Chicago: Rand McNally, 1976.

Bennis, W. G. *Changing Organizations: Essays on the Development and Evolution of Human Organizations*. New York: McGraw-Hill, 1966.

Bennis, W. G. *Organization Development: Its Nature, Origins and Prospects*. Reading, Mass.: Addison-Wesley, 1969.

Brief, A. P., Aldag, R. J., and Jacox, A. The impact of task characteristics on employee responses in hospital nursing. *Nursing Administration Quarterly*, in press.

Caro, F. G. *Readings in Evaluation Research*. New York: Russell Sage Foundation, 1971.

Cook, T. D., and Campbell, D. T. The design and conduct of quasi-experiments and true experiments in field settings. In *Handbook of Industrial and Organizational Psychology*, ed. by M. D. Dunnette. Chicago: Rand McNally, 1976.

Evans, M. G. The moderating effects of internal versus external control on the relationship between various aspects of job satisfaction. *Studies in Personnel Psychology, 5*, 1973, 37–46.

Frank, L. L., and Hackman, J. R. A failure of job enrichment: The case of the change that wasn't. *Journal of Applied Behavioral Science, 11*, 1975, 413–36.

Golembiewski, R. T., Hilles, R., and Kagno, M. A longitudinal study of flexitime effects: Some consequences of an OD structural intervention. *Journal of Applied Behavioral Science*, 10, 1974, 503–32.

Golembiewski, R. T., Yeager, S., and Hilles, R. Factor analysis of some flexitime effects: Attitudinal and behavioral consequences of a structural intervention. *Academy of Management Journal*, 18, 1975, 500–509.

Guttentag, M., and Struening, E. L. *Handbook of Evaluation Research*, Vol. 2. Beverly Hills, Calif.: Sage, 1976.

Hackman, J. R., and Lawler, E. E., III. Employee reactions to job characteristics. *Journal of Applied Psychology Monograph*, 55, 1971, 259–86.

Hackman, J. R., and Oldham, G. R. Development of the Job Diagnostic Survey. *Journal of Applied Psychology*, 60, 1975, 159–70.

Holly, W. H., Armenakis, A. A., and Field, H. S. Employee reactions to a flexitime program: A longitudinal study. *Human Resources Management*, 15, 1976, 21–23.

Latham, G. P., and Yukl, G. A. A review of research on the application of goal setting in organizations. *Academy of Management Journal*, 18, 1975, 824–45.

Laufer, A. C. *Operations Management*. Cincinnati: South-Western Publishing Co., 1975.

Lawler, E. E., III. Job design and employee motivation. *Personnel Psychology*, 22, 1969, 426–35.

Lawler, E. E., III, Hackman, J. R., and Kaufman, S. Effects of job redesign: A field experiment. *Journal of Applied Social Psychology*, 3, 1973, 49–62.

Locke, E. A. Toward a theory of task motivation and incentives. *Organizational Behavior and Human Performance*, 3, 1968, 157–89.

Locke, E. A., Cartledge, N., and Knerr, C. S. Studies of the relationship between satisfaction, goal-setting, and performance. *Organizational Behavior and Human Performance*, 5, 1970, 135–58.

Locke, E. A., Cartledge, N., and Koeppel, J. Motivational effects of knowledge of results: A goal-setting phenomenon. *Psychological Bulletin*, 70, 1968, 474–85.

McCormick, E. J. The development of processes for indirect or synthetic validity: III. Application of job analysis to indirect validity: A symposium. *Personnel Psychology*, 12, 1959, 402–13.

McCormick, E. J. Job and task analysis. In *Handbook of Industrial and Organizational Psychology,* ed. by M. D. Dunnette. Chicago: Rand McNally, 1976.

McCormick, E. J., Jeanneret, P. R., and Mecham, R. C. A study of job characteristics and job dimensions as based on the Position Analysis Questionnaire (PAQ). *Journal of Applied Psychology Monograph, 56,* 1972, 347-68.

Macy, B. A., and Mirvis, P. H. A methodology for assessment of quality of work life and organizational effectiveness in behavioral-economic terms. *Administrative Science Quarterly, 21,* 1976, 212-26.

Mirvis, P. H., and Lawler, E. E., III. Measuring the financial impact of employee attitudes. *Journal of Applied Psychology, 62,* 1977, 1-8.

Mirvis, P. H., and Macy, B. A. Human resource accounting: A measurement perspective. *Academy of Management Review, 1,* 1976, 74-83.

Morsh, J. E., and Archer, W. B. *Procedural Guide for Conducting Occupational Surveys in the United States Air Force.* Lackland Air Force Base, Texas: Personnel Research Laboratory, Aerospace Medical Division, PRL-TR-67-11, September, 1967.

Partridge, B. E. Notes on the impact of flexitime in a large insurance company: II. Reactions of supervisors and managers. *Occupational Psychology, 47,* 1973, 241-42.

Pierce, J. L., and Dunham, R. B. Task design: A literature review. *The Academy of Management Review, 1,* 1976, 83-97.

Prien, E. P., and Ronan, W. W. Job analysis: A review of research findings. *Personnel Psychology, 24,* 1971, 371-96.

Rhode, J. G., and Lawler, E. E., III. Auditing change: Human resource accounting. In *Work and Nonwork in the Year 2001,* ed. by M. D. Dunnette. Monterey, Calif.: Brooks/Cole, 1973.

Salancik, G. R., and Pfeffer, J. An alternative perspective on job attitudes and task design I: A review and critique of the need satisfaction model. Unpublished manuscript, University of Illinois, 1976.

Schein, E. H. *Process Consultation: Its Role in Organizational Development.* Reading, Mass.: Addison-Wesley, 1969.

Schein, E. H., and Bennis, W. G. *Personal and Organizational Change Through Group Methods: The Laboratory Approach.* New York: Wiley, 1965.

Schwab, D. P., and Cummings, L. L. A theoretical analysis of the impact of task scope on employee performance. *The Academy of Management Review, 1,* 1976, 23–35.

Sims, H. P., Jr., Szilagyi, A. D., and Keller, R. T. The measurement of job characteristics. *Academy of Management Journal, 19,* 1976, 195–212.

Smith, P. C., Kendall, L. M., and Hulin, C. L. *The Measurement of Satisfaction in Work and Retirement.* Chicago: Rand McNally, 1969.

Staw, B. M. *Intrinsic and Extrinsic Motivation.* Morristown, N.J.: General Learning Press, 1976.

Steers, R. M., and Mowday, R. T. The motivational properties of tasks. Unpublished manuscript, University of Oregon, 1976.

Suchman, E. A. *Evaluative Research; Principles and Practice in Public Service and Social Action Programs.* New York: Russell Sage Foundation, 1967.

Tiffin, J., and McCormick, E. J. *Industrial Psychology.* 5th ed. Englewood Cliffs, N.J.: Prentice-Hall, 1965.

Umstot, D. D., Bell, C. H., and Mitchell, T. R. Effects of job enrichment and task goals on satisfaction and productivity: Implications for job design. *Journal of Applied Psychology, 61,* 1976, 379–94.

Individual and Situational Factors in Job Redesign

5

Anyone who has read Studs Terkel's series of interviews, *Working* (1972), has to be struck by the different ways in which people view their work, in terms of the aspects of work they consider important and of their reactions to job characteristics. A former quiz kid who has gone through a succession of jobs likes his current work in a greenhouse because his mind is at ease all day long. Conversely, a garbage collector keeps his mind occupied by analyzing how families live on the basis of what they throw out. Some workers are willing to put up with monotonous jobs in order to make money to do other things. A cab driver says his work is just a way to get enough money to buy a car wash and, ultimately, to buy a schooner he'll charter in the West Indies. Other workers stress job ease. A fashion model feels guilty because she is spending her life doing something she doesn't like. "It's not very fulfilling," she says, ". . . but I'm lazy, I admit it. It's an easier thing to do" (p. 54). Still others find a variety of ways to make their jobs more meaningful. An elevator starter has assumed security functions and acts as an information source, giving room numbers. A steelworker sometimes deliberately dents his work as a way of making an imprint that he can recognize as his own. Employees also differ both in the ways they perceive the status of various jobs and in their reactions to those perceptions. A janitor lies to his old friends about what he does for a living, claiming that he's a lawyer. A prostitute talks of the differences in image and expectations at various levels of the prostitution status hierarchy. A grave digger complains that his work is looked down upon by most people but really requires a variety of skills and is important because "when these people is buried, he's buried for life" (p. 508).

These comments suggest that individuals are likely to respond in very different ways to particular task attributes, and consequently, to changes in such characteristics. Differences in attitudes toward work and toward job characteristics are evident at a variety of levels, from individual to cultural. Hulin (1971) points out that anthropological literature reveals striking differences in the meaning of work from culture to culture:

> For example, among the Tikopeans of Oceania, work as a general concept is "good" and idleness is an evil similar to a religious offense. The people of Tikopea start work early, take few breaks and often compete with each other to see who can accomplish the most . . . On the other hand, work is but a necessary evil for the Siriono of the Amazon Basin. They work when absolutely necessary, and only to obtain food. When food is available, they rest and there are no group or cultural sanctions for idleness (pp. 168-69).

In view of these differences in work attitudes between both individuals and groups, it becomes important to consider whether a particular work force may desire certain types of job characteristics. Chapter 4 stressed that an assessment of need should be undertaken prior to the implementation of a job redesign program. This chapter considers what specific factors should be examined during need assessment. Evidence concerning individual and group differences in perceptions of and reactions to job characteristics, as well as situational factors which might influence the effectiveness of job redesign, will be examined. That evidence provides useful clues concerning particular individual differences and contextual characteristics which should be assessed prior to major job redesign.

URBANIZATION

Early research into the impact of individual differences on reactions to task characteristics focused upon sociological moderators.[1] As noted in Chapter 3, Turner and Lawrence's major 1965 study of attitudinal and behavioral responses of employees to task characteristics laid the groundwork for much recent research. They expected to find positive responses to high-level jobs, characterized by high degrees of autonomy, complexity, variety, and so on. Instead, they found that while workers from factories in small towns acted in expected ways, those from large cities showed dissatisfaction with supposedly desirable job attributes and satisfaction with such a supposedly undesirable attribute as repetitiveness. Turner and Lawrence reasoned that workers in large cities were likely to be normless because of the very heterogeneous social cultures in such cities. That is, they would be unlikely to develop strong group or subcultural norms and values because of the size and variety of the population. As a result, they would not possess white-collar work values and would therefore be unlikely to respond well to challenging, skilled, autonomous jobs.

Blood and Hulin (1967) felt that such an interpretation was unwarranted. They argued that while workers from large cities may not share the work norms and values of the middle class, it should not be concluded that they have no norms. Indeed, in view of the fact that the fathers and grandfathers of the work-

---

[1]*A moderator is a variable that influences the relationship between other variables. For example, age may moderate the relationship between retirement benefits and satisfaction with the company's compensation package. The determination of moderating effects can be tricky (cf. Zedeck, 1971). In the area of job design, this has resulted in serious disputes. Some writers feel that the best way to assess such effects is by examining differences between subgroups formed on the basis of the moderator candidate, while others argue in favor of what are termed moderated regression techniques. Unfortunately, use of these alternative approaches can lead to markedly different results.*

ers surveyed by Turner and Lawrence had probably worked at unskilled or semiskilled jobs with little if any advancement, it would be surprising if those workers would adhere to the tenets of the Protestant work ethic.

To examine this issue, Blood and Hulin (1967) reanalyzed data collected and later published by Smith, Kendall, and Hulin (1969) from nineteen-hundred male workers in twenty-one plants in the eastern United States. Blood and Hulin classified the twenty-one plants according to six dimensions (slum conditions, urbanization, urban growth, prosperity and cost of living, productive farming, and population density) which they felt would foster alienation of blue-collar workers from middle-class work norms. They found that job level and work satisfaction were essentially unrelated in the community which possessed characteristics deemed likely to result in the most alienation. Conversely, workers from the most *integrated* (that is, least alienating) community exhibited a moderately strong positive relationship between those variables. Blood and Hulin concluded that:

> ... the best job design in alienating conditions may be contrary to the models usually proposed by human-relations–oriented investigators. Although integrated workers desire greater responsibility and autonomy, alienated workers may be happiest when given a job which demands little personal involvement either in terms of task skills or identification with the goals of management (p. 289).

Blood and Hulin felt that by considering indices of alienation, it would be possible to make improved predictions about how workers would be likely to respond to job characteristics. They also argued that by focusing on such indices, it would be unnecessary to ask workers directly about what types of jobs they would prefer.

Hulin and Blood (1968) reviewed the literature to that date bearing on the job enlargement thesis and relating job behavior and satisfaction.[2] Expanding on the Blood and Hulin

---

[2]*Other data suggesting that only certain segments of the working population might respond well to job enrichment are presented by Conant and Kilbridge (1965); Katzell, Barrett, and Parker (1961); Kendall (1963); Kennedy and O'Neill (1958); Kilbridge (1970); Kornhauser (1965); and Whyte (1955).*

(1967) contentions, they argued that many workers—in particular, white-collar workers and those blue-collar workers in small towns—would be integrated with and accept middle-class work norms. Such workers would be expected to respond positively to responsibility, variety, and so on. On the other hand, blue-collar workers from urban areas would be expected to be alienated from middle-class work norms and to respond negatively to enriched jobs.

While this model is appealing, and while results of some early studies were viewed as consistent with the model, most recent evidence fails to support it.[3] Recent researchers employing a wide variety of urbanization indices have generally failed to isolate significant differences in reactions to task characteristics consistent with the Hulin and Blood (1968) arguments.[4] In fact, some findings have been in the opposite direction from that which the Hulin and Blood model would predict (e.g., Aldag and Brief, 1975a).[5]

Thus, while Blood and Hulin (1967) argued that use of indices of alienation was preferable to direct measurement of employee desires, it appears that alienation indices have not lived up to their early promise.

ADHERENCE TO PROTESTANT WORK ETHIC

Since Hulin and Blood (1968) viewed urbanization indices as reflective of the probable degree to which an individual would adopt Protestant work ethic ideals, it was a natural step to consider directly the impact of adherence to Protestant work ethic ideals on reactions to task characteristics.[6]

Blood (1969) developed a scale, presented in Table 5—1, to

[3]For a review of studies which might be interpreted as supportive of the model, see Hulin (1971).
[4]Those indices include size of community of socialization or of plant location, congruence of urbanization of area of socialization with urbanization of current plant location, and self-reports of urbanization of area of socialization and of place of current residence.
[5]For one recent review of this literature, see Stone (1976).
[6]For some discussions of the Protestant work ethic, see Lenski (1961); Simpkins (1973); Weber (1958); and Wollack, Goodale, Wijting, and Smith (1971).

TABLE 5—1   Items to Measure Adherence to Protestant Work
                Ethic Ideals

Hard work makes a man a better person.
Wasting time is as bad as wasting money.
A good indication of a man's worth is how well he does his job.
If all other things are equal, it is better to have a job with a lot of
  responsibility than one with little responsibility.

From Blood (1969).

measure the extent to which an individual adheres to Protestant
work ethic ideals. Blood theorized that such adherence would be
a reflection of the belief that hard work results in desirable out-
comes, that good work is indicative of personal worth, and that
responsibility is desirable.[7]

       There is some evidence to suggest that employees strongly
adhering to the Protestant work ethic are more satisfied with
their work than are others (e.g., Aldag and Brief, 1975c; Blood,
1969). But while it certainly makes sense to argue that someone
responding positively to items such as those on the Blood scale
would be likely to react favorably to work *in general*, it is not so
clear why he or she would necessarily value autonomy, variety,
and the other core task dimensions. Blood himself notes that "a
person who feels that personal worth results only from self-sac-
rificing work or occupational achievement would likely derive
some satisfaction even in a demanding menial position" (p. 456).
Consequently, it might be expected that measures of adherence
to the Protestant work ethic would be useful in predicting satis-
faction with work in general but would not be of much value in
predicting responses to particular job characteristics.

       In fact, most evidence concerning the role of the Protestant
work ethic does not support the contention that employees' re-
sponses to job characteristics differ significantly as a function of
the degree to which they adhere to the tenets of the Protestant
work ethic.[8] On the basis of his research and literature review,
Stone (1976) has argued that the "Protestant ethic is probably *not*

---

[7]*For evidence relating to properties and correlates of this scale, see Aldag and
Brief (1975b). For other scales to assess adherence to the Protestant work
ethic, see Mirels and Garrett (1971) and Wollack, Goodale, Wijting, and
Smith (1971).*
[8]*For a critical review of relevant literature, see Stone (1976).*

an important individual difference variable to consider when the researcher or practitioner is concerned with how satisfaction with the work itself will be influenced by changes in job scope" (p. 164), and that "efforts aimed at increasing the scope of workers' jobs (e.g., job enrichment) will be reacted to no less positively by alienated than by integrated workers" (p. 164).

The lesson that emerges from the literature reviewed to this point is that it is dangerous to predict how workers will respond to tasks on the basis of crude community-level measures or even of more micro-level indices, such as adherence to Protestant work ethic ideals, which fail to assess directly desires for particular job characteristics. A more promising alternative is offered by direct assessment of employee needs.

HIGHER-ORDER NEED STRENGTH

The model of employee reactions to their jobs which was presented in Chapter 4 showed that such reactions are a function of task attribute perceptions, valences attached to those task attributes, and instrumentalities of the task attributes. Consequently, it would seem that assessment of the valences an employee attaches to specific enriched job attributes would provide the most direct and meaningful measure of readiness for job redesign.[9]

In Chapter 2, we discussed Alderfer's scheme of need categorization. The reader will recall that Alderfer classified needs as focusing on existence, relatedness, or growth. *Growth-needs* were defined as those needs for enhancement of one's creative or productive potential. It seems reasonable to expect that employees with strong growth-needs would be more likely to respond positively to enriched job characteristics than would others. That is, responsibility, autonomy, variety, and so on should be positively valent for such employees.

Consistent with these ideas, a recent focus of task design research has been on the role of needs similar to Alderfer's growth-needs. Since such needs roughly correspond to those at

[9]For one attempt to relate job characteristics directly to expectancy theory measures, see Sims and Szilagyi (1976).

the highest levels in Maslow's need hierarchy, most researchers have in their work written in terms of higher-order need strength. Examinations of the role of higher-order need strength have generally not focused directly on the strength of such variables as the need for self-actualization or the need for autonomy, but rather have considered desires for job characteristics which would seem likely to satisfy such needs.[10] Since it is actually the strength of desires for specific job characteristics which would appear to be most relevant, such a focus is appropriate.[11]

One widely used scale for assessing preferences for specific job characteristics was developed by Hackman and Oldham (1974). That scale, entitled *Higher-Order Need Strength Measure B,* is presented in Table 5—2.[12] Relative strength of growth-needs is reflected in the choice of jobs characterized by opportunities for participation in decision making, use of a variety of valued skills and abilities, freedom and independence, challenge, expression of creativity, and opportunity for learning, over those stressing high pay, fringe benefits, job security, friendly co-workers, and considerate supervision.

Quite a bit of evidence has now accumulated to suggest that higher-order need strength, at least as reflected in preferences for jobs that should satisfy higher-order needs, may be an important determinant of the way an employee will respond to enriched task characteristics. For example, Hackman and Lawler (1971), in a study discussed in detail in Chapter 4, found a more positive relationship between employee satisfaction and other responses and such task dimensions as skill variety and autonomy for employees characterized by strong higher-order need strength as gauged by their scale than for those with weaker higher-order need strength.[13]

At this point in the evolution of job design research, it

[10]For one study that did consider directly the moderating effects of such needs, see Stone, Mowday, and Porter (in press).
[11]Wanous (1974) has argued that a developmental sequence may exist, with urbanization impacting on general work values, which in turn influence desires for specific job characteristics. However, recent research, and some of Wanous' own data, do not support such a sequence.
[12]An alternative measure of higher-order need strength developed by Hackman and Lawler (1971), entitled Higher-Order Need Strength Measure A, appears to have generally less desirable properties than Measure B. For an examination of these scales, see Aldag and Brief (1977a).
[13]For survey or experimental replications of this finding, see Brief and Aldag (1975b); Robey (1974); and Sims and Szilagyi (1976).

appears that attempts to measure the valence of enriched job characteristics directly, such as that of Hackman and Oldham, provide the most promising means of determining whether current or potential incumbents of target jobs would be amenable to job enrichment.

SEX, RACE, AND AGE

To this point we have reviewed evidence concerning a number of potential moderators of the impact of task characteristics on employee responses. Each of those potential moderators was initially selected for study because reasonable arguments could be made for why it should play a direct or indirect role in influencing reactions of employees to their jobs. A number of other variables have been considered, not so much because of any compelling reason to believe that they should play a moderating role, but rather because they are readily visible and are commonly used to classify people in everyday life. Three such variables are sex, race, and age.

Many writers have argued that women are more concerned with social aspects of jobs than are men, while men are relatively more interested in pay, advancement, and freedom on the job.[14] If such differences do exist, it would seem to follow that males would be more suitable candidates for most job enrichment attempts than would females. It is generally suggested that such differences are the result of socialization processes. Vroom (1964) states:

> The different values and occupational choices of men and women undoubtedly stem, at least in part, from differing patterns of socialization. Conceivably, boys, through identification with their fathers, are more likely to learn the desirability of being a "good provider" for one's family, while girls may be more likely to acquire the "socio-emotional" concerns of their mothers (p. 93).

[14]For example, see Centers and Bugental (1966); Converse and Robinson (1972); Hardin, Reif, and Heneman (1951); and Gurin (1970). For a review of studies concerning sex-related and race-related differences in occupational attitudes, see Brief and Aldag (1975a).

TABLE 5—2   Higher-Order Need Strength Measure B

INSTRUCTIONS

People differ in what they like and dislike in their jobs. For each pair, you are to indicate which job you would prefer. Listed below are twelve pairs of jobs. For each pair, you are to indicate which job you would prefer. Assume that everything else about the jobs is the same—pay attention only to the characteristics actually listed for each pair of jobs.

If you would prefer the job in the left-hand column (Column A), indicate how much you prefer it putting a check mark in a blank to the left of the "neutral" point. If you prefer the job in the right-hand column (Column B), check one of the blanks to the right of "neutral." Check the "neutral" blank only if you find the two jobs equally attractive or unattractive. Try to use the "neutral" blank rarely.

COLUMN A	Strongly prefer A		Neutral		Strongly prefer B	COLUMN B
1. A job which offers little or no challenge.						A job which requires you to be completely isolated from co-workers.
2. A job where the pay is very good.						A job where there is considerable opportunity to be creative and innovative.
3. A job where you are often required to make important decisions.						A job with many pleasant people to work with.
4. A job with little security in a somewhat unstable organization.						A job in which you have little or no opportunity to participate in decisions which affect your work.
5. A job in which greater responsibility is given to those who do the best work.						A job in which greater responsibility is given to loyal employees who have the most seniority.

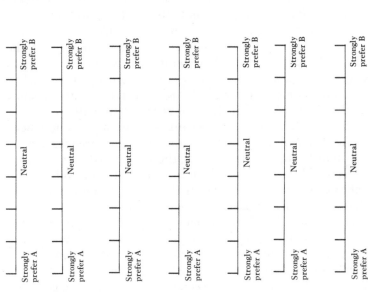

6. A job with a super-
visor who sometimes is
highly critical.

Strongly
prefer A

Neutral

Strongly
prefer B

A job which does not
require you to use much
of your talent.

7. A very routine job.

Strongly
prefer A

Neutral

Strongly
prefer B

A job where your co-
workers are not very
friendly.

8. A job with a super-
visor who respects
you and treats you
fairly.

Strongly
prefer A

Neutral

Strongly
prefer B

A job which provides
constant opportunities
for you to learn new
and interesting things.

9. A job where you have
a real chance to
develop yourself
personally.

Strongly
prefer A

Neutral

Strongly
prefer B

A job with excellent
vacations and fringe
benefits.

10. A job where there is a
real chance you could
be laid off.

Strongly
prefer A

Neutral

Strongly
prefer B

A job with very little
chance to do challenging
work.

11. A job with little free-
dom and independence
to do your work in the
way you think best.

Strongly
prefer A

Neutral

Strongly
prefer B

A job where the working
conditions are poor.

12. A job with very
satisfying team-work.

Strongly
prefer A

Neutral

Strongly
prefer B

A job which allows you
to use your skills and
abilities to the fullest
extent.

From Hackman and Oldham (1974).

While such arguments seem reasonable, there are at least two major reasons why it may be unwise to place undue weight on possible sex differences in occupational attitudes. First, we are seeing increasing pressure to reduce sex-role stereotyping. To the extent that such pressures are successful, historical socialization patterns will become less relevant. Second, many apparent differences between occupational preferences of males and females may simply reflect different job demands they face. For example, women may typically hold jobs characterized by relatively high demands for social interaction and offering relatively little opportunity for advancement. Brief, Rose, and Aldag (in press) examined this possibility using a stratified sample representative of the adult noninstitutionalized population of the continental United States. They found that when occupational category was controlled for, there were no significant sex differences in importance rankings of high income, security, short hours, advancement, and feelings of accomplishment.

Little evidence exists to permit even tentative conclusions about relevant differences in occupational preferences among races. As pointed out by Ash (1972), there has until very recently been a "color-blind constraint" on most industrial psychological research. Consequently, there is little in the literature to guide the job designer on the basis of race of employees.

There appears to be a common acceptance of the view that desires for enriched task characteristics are largely confined to restless, well-educated younger employees. Older employees, raised in more austere times, are seen as placing relatively more importance on high pay and job security. This would suggest that job enrichment efforts should be directed toward the young, while the desires of an older work force could be better met by focusing on extrinsic rewards. However, the scanty evidence regarding this issue does not support such a contention. Aldag and Brief (1975c) examined two samples of employees, one from a manufacturing firm and the other from a public sector service agency, and found few significant differences between the ways that younger and older workers responded to perceptions of task dimensions.

In summary, the evidence concerning the roles of sex, race, and age serves to reinforce the contention made earlier that it is generally unnecessary and unwise to use crude proxies for what employees might want from their jobs. Instead, direct assessment of individual desires is preferable.

PERCEPTION OF OBJECTIVE TASK CHARACTERISTICS

To this point, the individual difference measures which have been considered are those which might influence the way the employee responds to individual perceptions of certain task characteristics. We have seen that there is fairly consistent evidence to suggest that employees with strong higher-order needs are likely to respond more favorably to enriched jobs than would their opposites. However, as we will see, it would appear that individual differences may also play another role in the overall process of employee response to task characteristics.

Hackman (1969) noted in his review of literature on tasks that individuals often substantially redefine tasks they are asked to perform, and that such redefinition is at least in part a function of differences in individuals' needs, values, and past experiences.[15] Thus, two individuals faced with the same job might perceive it very differently in terms of skill variety, task significance, and so on. For example, someone who has had many years of experience on a given job might view the job as more routine than would an individual newly faced with the task. Likewise, someone with years of training and education in a given area might see a particular low-level job as boring and insignificant, while a less trained employee might perceive the job as challenging and important. Consequently, as shown in Figure 5—1, individual differences are likely to moderate both the linkage between objective task characteristics and perceptions of the job and the linkage between those perceptions and employee responses. Further, very different individual difference measures may be relevant at the two points in the process.

To test the possibility that various individuals might perceive the same task to possess different levels of the core task dimensions, Stone (1977) had students perform a simple assembly task and then fill out questionnaires concerning their perceptions of the task characteristics and satisfaction with the task. In addition, the students completed other instruments which assessed personality characteristics. Stone found that, even though the task was identical for all students, there were significant differences in perceptions of such task dimensions as variety,

[15]For one review of individual differences as correlates of perceptions of and reactions to stimuli, see Stone (1977).

FIGURE 5—1   Moderating Roles of Individual Differences

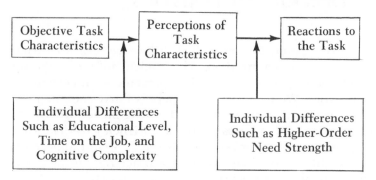

autonomy, task identity, and feedback as a function of such vari-
ables as age, cognitive structure, and dominance. In other words,
people with different histories, ways of thinking, and traits saw
the same task in different ways.

In a similar vein, Aldag and Brief (1977b), using a sample
of hospital employees, examined how the relationships between
sets of behaviors required on the job and perceptions of the core
task dimensions differed as a function of educational level and
other variables. They found that while employees with high edu-
cation levels saw strong relationships between apparently com-
plex, enriched behaviors and the core task dimensions, those
employees with relatively little education viewed apparently
routine behaviors as being relatively high in the core task dimen-
sions.[16] Aldag and Brief concluded that as jobs become objec-
tively more varied and complex, employees perceive them as be-
ing more and more enriched only up to a certain point. Beyond
that point, additional increases in objective complexity, variety,
and so on might result in confusion and feelings of incompetence.
Further, the levels above which such confusion may result are
probably a function of such individual differences as education
level, amount of training, and intelligence. Consequently, as was
stressed in Chapter 4, it is important to measure what employees
perceive the current levels of task dimensions to be and to learn

[16]*Aldag and Brief also found that the time the employee had spent on the
current job influenced the relationship between required job behaviors and
perceptions of the core task dimensions. For another study showing tenure to
be a relevant determinant of responses to job changes, see Lawler, Hackman,
and Kaufman (1973).*

how objective task characteristics are related to such perceptions. Without such information, attempts at job redesign must be based largely on guesswork and may lead to unexpected, undesirable outcomes.

PHYSICAL CHARACTERISTICS AND PHYSIOLOGICAL RESPONSES

The previous sections considered the relevance to job design of such factors as the employee's area of socialization, work values, preferences for particular job outcomes, and demographic characteristics. This section briefly examines the need to assess workers' physical characteristics and physiological responses. While such factors are less relevant to the specific issue of job enrichment than are employee occupational preferences, they should be considered in the overall design of the job. Among such variables are anthropometric factors, neuromuscular factors, strength and endurance, body cycles, energy expenditures, and fatigue.[17]

Anthropometric factors

Anthropometry is the name given to evaluation of human body measurements. On some dimensions (such as buttock-knee length) there is much less variability among individuals than on others (such as weight). Body measurements vary substantially with sex, age, race, and occupation. Anthropometric data is useful for many purposes, such as designing the *work-space envelope* of the worker, determining optimal dimensions and contours of work surfaces, designing controls, and so on. In some cases, it is possible to design the job to fit the hypothetical "average" person; in others, it may be necessary to accommodate individuals with even the most extreme dimensions or to allow flexibility to adjust for individuals of various dimensions.

[17]*Two journals devoted to these topics are* Ergonomics, *published in England, and* Human Factors, *published in the United States.*

Neuromuscular factors

Some jobs require the worker to carry out a sequence of motions in conjunction with the senses. Such tasks, called *sensory-motor tasks,* place great emphasis on the worker's perceptual abilities. For example, Laufer (1975) notes that most assembly operations, clerical activities, and many other white-collar jobs fall into this category. Our senses include hearing, sight, touch, smell, and taste, each of which may be more or less important for particular tasks. When it is desired to speed up the employee's response time on a task, we should see that stimuli are presented in a clear and unambiguous manner, that the number of alternatives from which to choose is minimized, and that advance warning of stimuli is given.[18]

Strength and endurance

For jobs requiring physical exertion, strength and endurance are clearly important. Some correlates of strength and endurance include:[19]

1. Age:
Strength reaches a maximum by the middle to late twenties and then continually declines until at age sixty-five it is about 75 percent of its maximum level. In general, however, continuous-work capacity of males doesn't appear to decrease with age, at least up to age sixty.
2. Sex:
Women's strength is about two thirds that of men.
3. Body Build:
While athletic-appearing individuals are stronger than others, less powerfully built individuals are more efficient. For rapidly fatiguing, severe exercise, slender individuals are best, while normal build is best for moderate exercise.
4. Exercise:
Exercise can increase strength and endurance as much as 30 to 50 percent above initial levels.

[18]*For more on this issue, see McCormick (1976).*
[19]*From McCormick (1976).*

Body cycles

We've all heard people talk about how their "body clocks" have been thrown out of kilter for some reason, such as a change in time zones.[20] In fact, it does seem that most bodily functions exert a regular variability relating to a twenty-four-hour cycle. Temperature, heart rate, brain-wave pattern, blood-cell counts, skin conductivity, and over forty other bodily functions show such diurnal (or circadian) biological rhythms.[21] Light, temperature, isolation, altered working hours, sleep loss, and a number of other factors can alter those cycles. Of these factors, light seems to be the most powerful, with biological rhythms being affected by changes in light-dark cycles in as little as three hours.

The rotation of employees from one shift to another can disturb these diurnal rhythms, in many cases causing fatigue, discomfort, digestive problems, and other undesirable consequences. Some bodily functions are slower in adapting than others, taking up to four days. Consequently, if shifts are changed regularly, the rhythm of certain bodily functions may be continually unstable. Some simple skill measures, such as reaction time, are found to deteriorate during adjustments to new cycles. However, mental and motor performance are apparently not related in any simple way to bodily rhythms.

Energy expenditures

Knowledge of energy expenditures can be used as a basis for figuring rest periods, time allowed for task completion, and so on. Among the objective measures of energy expenditures are oxygen consumption, heart rate, recordings of electrical impulses occurring during work in specific muscles, and irregularity of heart action.[22]

Fatigue

If energy expenditures exceed certain limits, fatigue may occur.[23] The likelihood of fatigue on the job is a function of a

[20]This information is drawn from Ferguson (1971).
[21]Trumbull (1966).
[22]For a fuller discussion of this issue, see McCormick (1976).
[23]For more on this issue, see Ferguson (1971).

number of factors in addition to job demands, such as environ-
mental conditions, machine design, personal fitness, and
psychological characteristics. Muscular fatigue results from se-
vere physical exertion, while skill fatigue is caused by continuous
performance of an activity. Repetitive work which requires rapid
hand and arm movements can result in either skill fatigue or local
muscular fatigue. Such fatigue may result in a falling off of out-
put, irregularity in the rate of output, and physical discomfort.
Consequently, repetitive work may result in reduced perfor-
mance because of both boredom and fatigue.

SITUATIONAL FACTORS

The model of employee responses outlined in Chapter 4
suggested that, in addition to perceptions of task characteristics,
the valences and instrumentalities attached to those characteris-
tics should also be key determinants of employee responses to the
job. We have now seen that people differ in the way they perceive
the same job and in the valences they attach to those perceptions.
We will now consider situational determinants of the valences
people attach to task characteristics and of their instrumentality
perceptions.

There are at least two situational factors which would
cause valences attached to enriched task characteristics to be
low. First, the characteristics may already be present at such
high levels in the job that desires for variety, autonomy, and other
enriched job dimensions would be well satisfied. In addition,
there is evidence to indicate that lower-order needs must be
reasonably well satisfied before higher-order needs become im-
portant.[24] Thus, if there is much dissatisfaction with extrinsic
factors, such as pay or supervision, it is unlikely that great em-
phasis will be placed on intrinsic job characteristics. There is
evidence to support each of these hypotheses.

A study by Sims and Szilagyi (1976) suggests that current
levels of core task dimensions may influence the desirability of
job enrichment. They surveyed over 1100 medical center
paramedical and support personnel concerning perceptions of job

[24]For instance, see Lawler and Suttle (1972) and Wahba and Bridwell
(1976).

characteristics, satisfaction, and other variables. The administrative group, at the highest occupational level, demonstrated significantly higher levels of variety and of dealing with others and lower levels of feedback and task identity than did those at lower occupational levels. Further, while variety and dealing with others were highly related to satisfaction for the lower occupational levels, the administrative group showed a weaker desire for those characteristics and a stronger desire for feedback. Sims and Szilagyi argued that the administrative group may already be overloaded with environmental complexity and therefore have little desire for more variety and interaction but great desire for feedback.

Work by Oldham (1976) supports the contention that when workers are dissatisfied with extrinsic factors, intrinsic job characteristics appear to be relatively unimportant. He found that employees who were satisfied with supervisors and co-workers showed strong, generally significant relationships between perceived levels of task dimensions and the extent to which they were internally motivated to perform well. Conversely, the internal motivation of employees who were dissatisfied with their supervisors and co-workers was not significantly related to task dimension perceptions. Oldham, Hackman, and Pearce (1976) found that employees who were satisfied with extrinsic factors (including pay, security, co-workers, and supervision) showed significant positive relationships between the level of enriched characteristics of their jobs and performance, salary (corrected for tenure), and internal work motivation. For employees who were dissatisfied with extrinsic factors, relationships were regularly weaker. The most favorable reactions to perceptions of enriched task characteristics were generally exhibited in employees characterized by both satisfaction with extrinsic factors and strong higher-order needs, while the least favorable reactions were exhibited by their opposites.

There is also evidence concerning situational determinants of instrumentality perceptions. Dunham (1977) has argued that:

> ... employees may or may not focus on task design as a function of non-task elements in the work environment. That is to say that although an employee's job may have an expanded task design, the worker does not experience

the psychological aspects (i.e., intrinsic outcomes) of expanded tasks because of distracting environmental factors (pp. 43-4).

Dunham explains this contention in terms of the expectancy model of motivation reviewed in Chapter 2. That is, while outcomes associated with enriched task characteristics may be valued by the employee, nontask environmental factors may actually "block" either attainment or cognition of those outcomes. Instrumentalities would thus be low. Based on data collected from a large number of employees in the corporate offices of a major retail merchandising corporation, Dunham showed that persons in some parts of the organization responded favorably to enriched task characteristics while persons in other parts did not. While Dunham was unable to isolate the specific cause of that moderating effect, he reasoned that distracting environmental factors may have played some role. Whatever their cause, the findings further support the need to consider organizational determinants of responses to job characteristics.

SUMMARY

The evidence presented in this chapter suggests that:

1. Attempts at enhancement of employee satisfaction and performance through enrichment of task characteristics are likely to meet with varying degrees of success as a function of individual differences between employees. Those individual differences are likely to influence both the way the employee perceives characteristics of a job and the way he or she responds to those perceptions.

2. Direct measures of preferences for job characteristics appear to be better predictors of reactions to enriched task characteristics than are such indirect indices as urbanization of area of socialization or adherence to middle-class work values.

3. Certain situational factors, such as current levels of core task dimensions and determinants of the degree to

which an employee focuses on the task, apparently influence the impact of task characteristics on employee responses.

4. Employees dissatisfied with extrinsic factors (e.g., pay and supervision) are unlikely to respond well to job enrichment attempts.

The implications of the findings presented in this chapter are entirely consistent with the arguments presented in Chapter 4. That is, prior to the decision to implement a job redesign program, an assessment of need should be undertaken. Variables influencing the need for enrichment include adequacy of extrinsic factors, current levels of the core task dimensions, and the characteristics of employee need structures. Each of those variables can be measured using instruments which are currently available. In particular, levels of the core task dimensions can be assessed by use of the Job Characteristic Inventory (see Chapter 4), satisfaction with job facets can be measured by the Job Descriptive Index (see Chapter 4), and employee higher-order need strength can be gauged by Higher-Order Need Strength Measure B (discussed earlier in this chapter). In many cases, such as when work is repetitive or requires frequent shift changes, worker physical characteristics and physiological responses should also be considered. If it is determined that employees exhibit strong higher-order need strength, that extrinsic rewards are adequate, and that the jobs under consideration for redesign are perceived as being deficient in terms of the core task dimensions, the probability of successful redesign efforts is significantly improved. If such a pattern is not evident, alternatives to job design should be carefully explored.

REFERENCES

Aldag, R. J., and Brief, A. P. Impact of individual differences on employee affective responses to task characteristics. *Journal of Business Research, 3,* 1975a, 311-22.

Aldag, R. J., and Brief, A. P. Some correlates of work values. *Journal of Applied Psychology, 60,* 1975b, 757-60.

Aldag, R. J., and Brief, A. P. Age and reactions to task charac-
teristics. *Industrial Gerontology*, 2, 1975c, 223-29.
Aldag, R. J., and Brief, A. P. Examination of a measure of higher
order need strength. *Proceedings of the 20th Annual Confer-
ence of the Midwest Division of the Academy of Management*,
1977a, 133-43.
Aldag, R. J., and Brief, A. P. Moderators of relationships of job
behaviors to perceptions of core task dimensions. *Proceed-
ings of the 8th Annual Midwest Conference of the American
Institute for Decision Sciences*, 1977b, 327-29.
Alderfer, C. P. *Existence, Relatedness, and Growth: Human Needs
in Organizational Settings*. New York: The Free Press, 1972.
Ash, P. Job satisfaction differences among women of different
ethnic groups. *Journal of Vocational Behavior*, 2, 1972,
495-507.
Blood, M. R. Work values and job satisfaction. *Journal of Applied
Psychology*, 53, 1969, 456-59.
Blood, M. R., and Hulin, C. L. Alienation, environmental
characteristics, and worker responses. *Journal of Applied
Psychology*, 51, 1967, 284-90.
Brief, A. P., and Aldag, R. J. Male-female differences in occupa-
tional attitudes within minority groups. *Journal of Voca-
tional Behavior*, 6, 1975a, 305-14.
Brief, A. P., and Aldag, R. J. Employee reactions to task charac-
teristics: A constructive replication. *Journal of Applied
Psychology*, 60, 1975b, 182-86.
Brief, A. P., Aldag, R. J., and Jacox, A. The impact of task
characteristics on employee responses in hospital nursing.
Nursing Administration Quarterly, in press.
Brief, A. P., Rose, G. L., and Aldag, R. J. Sex differences in work
attitudes revisited. *Journal of Applied Psychology*, in press.
Centers, R., and Bugental, D. Intrinsic and extrinsic job motiva-
tions among different segments of the working population.
Journal of Applied Psychology, 50, 1966, 193-97.
Conant, E. H., and Kilbridge, M. D. An interdisciplinary analysis
of job enlargement: Technology, costs, and behavioral im-
plications. *Industrial and Labor Relations Review*, 18, 1965,
377-95.
Converse, P., and Robinson, J. The structure and meaning of time
use. In *The Use of Time*, ed. by A. Szalai et al. The Hague:
Mouton, 1972.

Dunham, R. B. Reactions to job characteristics: Moderating effects of the organization. *Academy of Management Journal*, 20, 1977, 42–65.

Ferguson, D. A. Fatigue and the organization of work. In *Introduction to Ergonomics: Special Readings*. Melbourne: Productivity Promotion Council of Australia, 1971.

Gurin, G. *A National Attitude Study of Trainees in MDTA Institutional Programs*. Ann Arbor: Survey Research Center, University of Michigan, 1970.

Hackman, J. R. Toward understanding the role of tasks in behavioral research. *Acta Psychologica*, 31, 1969, 97–128.

Hackman, J. R., and Lawler, E. E. III. Employee reactions to job characteristics. *Journal of Applied Psychology*, 55, 1971, 259–86.

Hackman, J. R., and Oldham, G. R. The Job Diagnostic Survey: An instrument for the diagnosis of jobs and the evaluation of job redesign projects. Technical Report No. 4, Department of Administrative Sciences, Yale University, May 1974.

Hardin, E., Reif, H. G., and Heneman, H. G. Stability of job preferences of department store employees. *Journal of Applied Psychology*, 35, 1951, 256–59.

Hulin, C. L. Individual differences and job enrichment—the case against general treatments. In *New Perspectives in Job Enrichment*, ed. by J. R. Maher. New York: Van Nostrand-Reinhold, 1971.

Hulin, C. L., and Blood, M. R. Job enlargement, individual differences, and worker responses. *Psychological Bulletin*, 69, 1968, 41–55.

Katzell, R. A., Barrett, R. S., and Parker, T. C. Job satisfaction, job performance, and situational characteristics. *Journal of Applied Psychology*, 45, 1961, 65–72.

Kendall, L. M. *Canonical Analysis of Job Satisfaction and Behavioral, Personal Background, and Situational Data*. Ph.D. dissertation, Cornell University, 1963.

Kennedy, J. E., and O'Neill, H. E. Job content and workers' opinions. *Journal of Applied Psychology*, 42, 1958, 372–75.

Kilbridge, M. D. Do workers prefer larger jobs? *Personnel*, 37, 1970, 45–48.

Kornhauser, A. W. *Mental Health of the Industrial Worker: A Detroit Study*. New York: Wiley, 1965.

Lawler, E. E. III, Hackman, J. R., and Kaufman, S. Effects of job redesign: A field experiment. *Journal of Applied Social Psychology, 3,* 1973, 49–62.

Lawler, E. E. III, and Suttle, J. L. A causal correlational test of the need hierarchy concept. *Organizational Behavior and Human Performance, 7,* 1972, 265–87.

Lenski, G. *The Religious Factor.* New York: Doubleday, 1961.

McCormick, E. J. *Human Factors in Engineering and Design.* New York: McGraw-Hill, 1976.

Mirels, H. L., and Garrett, J. B. The Protestant Ethic as a personality variable. *Journal of Consulting and Clinical Psychology, 36,* 1971, 40–44.

Oldham, G. R. Job characteristics and internal motivation: The moderating effect of interpersonal and individual variables. *Human Relations, 29,* 1976, 559–69.

Oldham, G. R., Hackman, J. R., and Pearce, J. L. Conditions under which employees respond positively to enriched work. *Journal of Applied Psychology, 61,* 1976, 395–403.

Robey, D. Task design, work values, and worker response: An experimental test. *Organizational Behavior and Human Performance, 12,* 1974, 264–73.

Schuler, R. Worker background and job satisfaction: A comment. *Industrial and Labor Relations Review, 26,* 1973, 851–53.

Shepard, J. Functional specialization, alienation, and job satisfaction. *Industrial and Labor Relations Review, 23,* 1970, 207–19.

Simpkins, E. The work ethic is not enough. *Monthly Labor Review, 96,* 1973, 59–60.

Sims, H. P., and Szilagyi, A. D. Job characteristics relationships: Individual and structural moderators. *Organizational Behavior and Human Performance, 17,* 1976, 211–30.

Smith, P. C., Kendall, L. M., and Hulin, C. L. *The Measurement of Satisfaction in Work and Retirement.* Chicago: Rand McNally, 1969.

Stone, E. F. The moderating effect of work-related values on the job scope–job satisfaction relationship. *Organizational Behavior and Human Performance, 15,* 1976, 147–67.

Stone, E. F. Some personality correlates of perceptions of and reactions to task characteristics. Working paper, Purdue University, 1977.

Stone, E. F., Mowday, R. T., and Porter, L. W. Higher-order need strengths as moderators of the job scope–job satisfaction relationship. *Journal of Applied Psychology,* in press.

Susman, G. I. Job enlargement: Effects of culture on worker responses. *Industrial Relations, 12,* 1973, 1–15.

Terkel, S. *Working.* New York: Pantheon, 1972.

Trumbull, R. Diurnal cycles and work-rest scheduling in unusual environments. *Human Factors, 8,* 1966, 385.

Turner, A. N., and Lawrence, P. R. *Industrial Jobs and the Worker: An Investigation of Response to Task Attributes.* Boston: Harvard University Press, 1965.

Vroom, V. H. *Work and Motivation.* New York: Wiley, 1964.

Wahba, M. A., and Bridwell, L. G. Maslow reconsidered: A review of research on the need hierarchy theory. *Organizational Behavior and Human Performance, 15,* 1976, 212–40.

Wanous, J. P. Individual differences and reactions to job characteristics. *Journal of Applied Psychology, 59,* 1974, 616–22.

Weber, M. *The Protestant Ethic and the Spirit of Capitalism.* Translated by T. Parsons. New York: Scribner, 1958.

Whyte, W. F. *Money and Motivation: An Analysis of Incentives in Industry.* New York: Harper, 1955.

Wollack, S., Goodale, J. G., Wijting, J. P., and Smith, P. C. Development of the survey of work values. *Journal of Applied Psychology, 55,* 1971, 331–38.

Zedeck, S. Problems with the use of "moderator" variables. *Psychological Bulletin, 76,* 1971, 295–310.

Organizational Factors in Job Redesign

6

It is increasingly recognized that there is no "one best" theory (any more than there is "one best" organization structure, form of leadership, or whatever) unless it is so general as to be of little utility in understanding the variety of organizations (Perrow, 1967, p. 204).

The basic function of administration appears to be co-alignment, not merely of people (in coalitions) but of institutionalized action—of technology and task environment into a viable domain, and of organizational design and structure appropriate to it (Thompson, 1967, p. 285).

... there can probably be no "one best" organizational structure or managerial orientation—not participative management, not bureaucracy, not any single fashionable methodology ... organizational success depends fundamentally upon meshing design (social technology) with the material technology out of which emerges the organization's tasks (Hunt, 1970, pp. 250–51).

[The contingency view] emphasizes the multivariate nature of or-

ganizations and attempts to understand how organizations operate under varying conditions and in specific circumstances. Contingency views are ultimately directed toward suggesting organizational designs and managerial systems most appropriate for specific situations (Kast and Rosenzweig, 1973, p. 51).

Early management theories espoused a "one best way" of doing things. But while it would be comforting to learn that a particular leadership style or organization design would be universally applicable, it is relatively easy to think of exceptions to almost any such general prescription. Instead, it is necessary to find the best approach for a given situation. This recognition has led to a growing number of *contingency* theories of organizational behavior and organization design. Such theories simply recognize that the best way to organize a company, to manage a subgroup, or to do almost anything in or with organizations may be dependent upon—that is, contingent upon—other factors. These theories essentially argue that there exists an optimal "fit" between variables.

In view of these contingency approaches, it would seem naive to expect that a single approach to job redesign—such as job enrichment—would be universally appropriate. We have already examined some relevant contingencies of task design as it relates to the individual employee. The previous chapter reviewed evidence indicating that the success of a job redesign intervention would be contingent upon such factors as the need structure of the work force, the current adequacy of extrinsic rewards, and the present levels of the core task dimensions. Further, we stressed that job changes should not be made without considering the characteristics of jobs surrounding those to be redesigned.

It seems reasonable to expect that the success of specific job redesign attempts is also a function of the general characteristics of the organization in which those attempts take place. For example, it seems obvious that the extent of an organization's reliance upon rules and regulations and upon formal communications channels would influence the degree to which management would resist enrichment efforts and target employees would doubt the sincerity of such efforts. Thus, there may be an optimal fit between task design and overall organization design.

ORGANIZATION DESIGN

It is quite easy to talk in generalities about organization design, but much more difficult to give the term concrete meaning. The reader can perhaps grasp this difficulty by thinking of all the ways in which any pair of firms may differ. Some important dimensions of organization design which have been frequently mentioned include the degree of formal structure within the organization, the extent to which decision-making is centralized, the distribution of rewards between organizational levels, and the relative size of the administrative component.[1] Different companies may exhibit entirely different combinations of these characteristics.

Classification of organization designs

Two essentially opposite patterns of organization characteristics were described by Burns and Stalker (1961). One pattern, which they called *mechanistic,* resembles in many ways a machine designed to maximize efficiency. The opposite pattern, *organic,* is more like a living organism, capable of flexibility and adaptability. Characteristics of these two types are presented in Table 6—1. The mechanistic organization possesses many of the attributes of what we generally think of as a bureaucracy, while the organic design is in many ways a reaction to presumed or demonstrated problems associated with the bureaucratic design.[2] It also seems likely that these aspects of organization design would influence the success of job redesign efforts. In particular, attempts at job enrichment in mechanistic firms would probably result in a variety of difficulties. It would be hard in

[1]*The term* organization climate *has sometimes been used as an aggregate label to encompass many different organization dimensions. For reviews of the climate literature and viewpoints concerning adequacy of the climate construct, see Guion (1973); Hellriegel and Slocum (1974); James and Jones (1974); Johannesson (1971, 1973); and Tagiuri (1969).*
[2]*There have been some questions about whether the characteristics which Burns and Stalker have associated with these types really do occur together. For example, Khandwalla (1974) has shown decentralization of top-level decision-making to be greatest in firms which the Burns and Stalker scheme would probably class as mechanistic.*

TABLE 6—1   Organic and Mechanistic Organization Designs

Organizational Characteristic	Type of Organization Design	
	Organic	Mechanistic
Specificity of required activities	Low	High
Content of communications	Advice and information	Instructions and decisions
Authority base	Knowledge	Position
Degree of decentralization in decision-making	High	Low
Levels of authority	Few	Many
Direction of interactions	Lateral, horizontal, and vertical	Vertical
Span of control	Wide	Narrow
Time span of employee discretion	Long	Short
Employee identification	With others in the organization	With others in the profession

Adapted from Burns and Stalker (1961).

such a firm for a manager—accustomed to giving orders, closely supervising, and relying on formal authority for legitimacy—to begin suddenly to delegate authority, play a more flexible supervisory role, and so on. Likewise, it would be hard for an employee whose job is redesigned to take seriously management's statements concerning worker autonomy and responsibility when confronted with the reality of a highly structured, rule-oriented organization design.[3]

Optimal organization design

One response to this difficulty of job enrichment in a mechanistic organization might be simply to argue that a mechanistic organization is generally undesirable and that in a properly designed, organic organization, job enrichment efforts would be universally appropriate. Argyris (1964), for example, has written of the dehumanizing influences of the bureaucratic

[3]For a discussion of other forces against job enrichment which arise in this sort of organization, see Perrow (1970).

FIGURE 6—1   The Argyris Maturity Drive Frustration Cycle

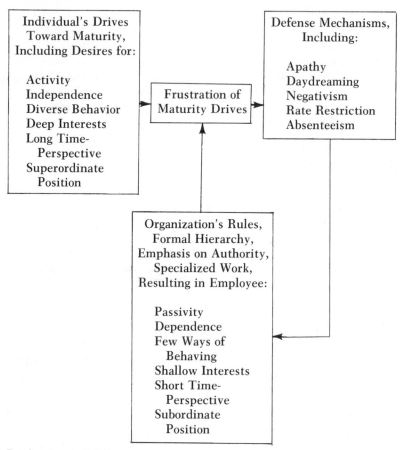

Based on Argyris (1964).

organization. His arguments are depicted in Figure 6—1. Basically, Argyris contends that healthy individuals have a variety of drives toward maturity. They want to be independent, to live actively rather than passively, and to explore numerous interests. The bureaucratic organization is seen by Argyris as demanding that employees adopt a pattern of interests, attitudes, and behaviors which are in conflict with those maturity drives. To reduce the frustration which results from this stifling of natural drives, employees engage in such defense mechanisms as apathy, negativism, and absenteeism. Argyris suggests that the response of the bureaucratic organization to such undesirable behaviors includes increased reliance upon rules, authority, formal organizational hierarchy, and so on. Thus, he contends, this self-reinforcing cycle of frustration makes the bureaucratic organization fundamentally inhospitable to healthy individuals.[4]

The bureaucratic organization has been criticized on a number of other grounds as well. It has been argued that bureaucracies ignore environmental demands and result in a variety of undesirable consequences, such as overreliance on rules and regulations, engagement in minimally acceptable behaviors, and overemphasis on the goals of the individual or subunit to the detriment of the overall goals of the organization.[5]

There are, however, at least two problems associated with trying to argue away the problem of task-organization fit by condemning the mechanistic organization. First, it may be impractical to change an organization from a mechanistic to an organic design. Thus, it may be necessary to design jobs within the constraints of a mechanistic organization. Further, it is simplistic to contend that a mechanistic structure is never appropriate. Rules and regulations, formal structure, and emphasis on authority all serve functions which are quite necessary in some situations.[6] For example, Filley (1976) has provided an interesting account of how differently a simple regulating device—a traffic light—was used in three instances. In one, it was an end in itself. In the second, it was used as a control device by an autocratic leader. In the third, it fostered an established pattern of traffic flow which allowed behavior to be predictable and actions to be coordinated. The moral Filley drew from his parable was that "when rules permit predictable behavior on routine issues, organization members can turn their attention to more significant problems" (p. 59).

In fact, there is now a growing body of evidence to suggest that mechanistic organizations may sometimes be quite appropriate, in terms of both organizational effectiveness and employee satisfaction. In particular, studies have shown that when firms are facing stable, predictable environments, it may be

---

[4]*It should be noted that Argyris recognizes only in passing the fact that some individuals may like routine jobs. He implies that those not desiring enriched jobs are by definition unhealthy, probably because previous experiences in bureaucratic organizations have stifled their maturity drives.*
[5]*For a detailed discussion of these problems, see March and Simon (1958).*
[6]*For a discussion of such functions, see Perrow (1970).*

possible to use the mechanistic form effectively. In such environments, demands for flexibility and adaptability are relatively low; thus the idea of treating the firm as a machine whose efficiency can be optimized without much consideration of outside forces becomes more possible. For example, Lawrence and Lorsch (1969) examined firms in three industries differing in the degree of uncertainty in their environments.[7] A major finding of their study was that successful firms were structured in such a way as to fit the demands of their environments. In general, successful firms facing certain environments tended to be more mechanistically structured, while high-performing firms in uncertain environments were more organically designed.

Morse (1970) extended these findings by looking at how the fit between organization design and the predictability of the organization's task related to organizational performance and individual motivation. His study considered four organizational units, two which performed the certain task of manufacturing standardized containers in one firm and two which carried out the uncertain task of research and development work in communication technology in another firm. In each pair of units, one was rated by management of the firm as a high performer and the other as a low performer. Characteristics of successful units facing each task are presented in Table 6—2.

It is evident that the successful unit facing certain task demands was highly structured, with tight control of behavior, little subordinate freedom, and a short time-orientation. Conversely, the successful unit performing the uncertain research task was more loosely structured, with more participative supervising and a long time-orientation. The low-performing container unit exhibited characteristics quite similar to those of the high-performing research laboratory, while the low-performing laboratory resembled the successful container unit. Further, Morse found that when there was a proper fit between the unit's

[7]Lawrence and Lorsch measured environmental uncertainty by looking at top executives' perceptions of the extent to which job requirements in various parts of the company were unclear, job accomplishment was difficult, and feedback concerning performance was slow. There have been some criticisms of the Lawrence and Lorsch measure of environmental uncertainty in particular and of reliance solely upon perceptual measures of the environment in general (cf. Aldag and Storey, 1975; and Tosi, Aldag, and Storey, 1973). Subsequent studies, however, have generally provided results consistent with the findings of Lawrence and Lorsch.

TABLE 6—2   Characteristics of Successful Units Facing Certain and Uncertain Tasks

	Akron (Certain Manufacturing Task)	Stockton (Uncertain Manufacturing Task)
1. Structural orientation	Perceptions of tightly controlled behavior and high degree of structure	Perceptions of low degree of structure
2. Time orientation	Short-term	Long-term
3. Goal orientation	Manufacturing	Scientific
4. Distribution of influence	Perceptions of low total influence, concentrated at upper levels	Perceptions of high total influence, more evenly spread out among all levels
5. Character of superior-subordinate relations	Low freedom vis-à-vis superiors to choose and handle task, directive type of supervision	High freedom vis-à-vis superiors to choose and handle task, participatory type of supervision
6. Character of colleague relations	Perceptions of much similarity among colleagues, high degree of coordination of colleague effort	Perceptions of much difference among colleagues, relatively low degree of coordination of colleague effort
7. Top executive's "managerial style"	More concerned with task than people	More concerned with task than people

From Morse (1970).

design and the demands of the unit's task, managers and professionals had higher feelings of *sense of competence motivation* than when the fit was improper. Such findings highlight the need to consider this fit between the organization, the individual, and the nature of the organization's task. In particular, they suggest that in some situations, a mechanistic structure may favorably influence both individual and organizational outcomes.

Another major study which indicates that no single organization design is universally appropriate was carried out by Woodward (1965) in the South Essex area of England. Her examination of 100 manufacturing firms showed that it was impossible to explain organizational design differences on the basis of such variables as company size, executive personality factors, or industry type. Company success also seemed unrelated to organizational design. Woodward then classified firms on the basis of their technologies into three major categories: small-batch and unit production, large-batch and mass production, and process or continuous production. As shown in Table 6—3, successful firms with large-batch or mass production technologies tended to have mechanistic designs, while high-performing firms with other technologies tended to be organic. There remain many questions regarding the explanations for Woodward's findings; but when coupled with those of Lawrence and Lorsch, they provide strong evidence that there may exist technological and environmental imperatives which dictate optimal organizational design.[8] It appears that when a product is mass-produced and the environment is such that demand is predictable, the emphasis of the organization is on efficiency. As such, a mechanistic design may be appropriate. On the other hand, when technology is more "made-to-order" and the environment makes demand unpredictable, the firm necessarily emphasizes creativity and adaptability. Consequently, an organic design would be desirable.

In short, there are reasons to believe that it may be infeasible or undesirable in some cases to adopt organic organization designs. Sometimes a mechanistic design may be more effective in achieving management's goals and in satisfying employees' needs. Thus it becomes necessary to address directly the question of proper task-organization fit.

[8]*For some other evidence relating to this issue, see Burns and Stalker (1961); Chandler (1962); Leavitt (1962); Stinchcombe (1959); and Udy (1959, 1964).*

TABLE 6—3   Technology and Successful Organization Design

Nature of Technology	Example of Technological Type	Predominant Design of Successful Firms
Small-batch and unit production	Production of special-purpose electronic equipment	Organic
Large-batch and mass production	Production of standard gasoline engines	Mechanistic
Process or continuous production	Production of chemicals, oil refining	Organic

Based on Woodward (1965).

Models of task-organization fit

One model which directly focuses on the interactions among individual needs, task attributes, and organization design has been presented by Porter, Lawler, and Hackman (1975). The model, shown in Figure 6—2, suggests that employees receive cues from both the overall organization and the job. The strength of individual growth (or higher-order) needs, the extent to which jobs are enlarged, and the degree to which the organization is organic are seen as the determinants of whether there is proper individual-task-organization *congruence* (that is, fit). Complete congruence occurs when either (a) high growth-need employees (as defined in Chapter 2) are working on enlarged jobs in organic organizations; or (b) low growth-need employees are working on routine jobs in mechanistic organizations. In both cases, the model predicts high performance, satisfaction, and attendance. Conversely, when either high growth-need employees are on routine jobs in mechanistic organizations, or low growth-need employees are on complex jobs in organic organizations, there would be a complete mismatch between the individual and the situation. The predicted result is the host of undesirable consequences noted in cells 1 and 8 of Figure 6—2. Finally, a mismatch may exist between the nature of the job and of the organization. In such cases, employees receive contradictory cues: while the general organization design sends one set of messages,

FIGURE 6—2   Predicted Relationships Among Organizational
Design, Job Design, and Employee Characteristics

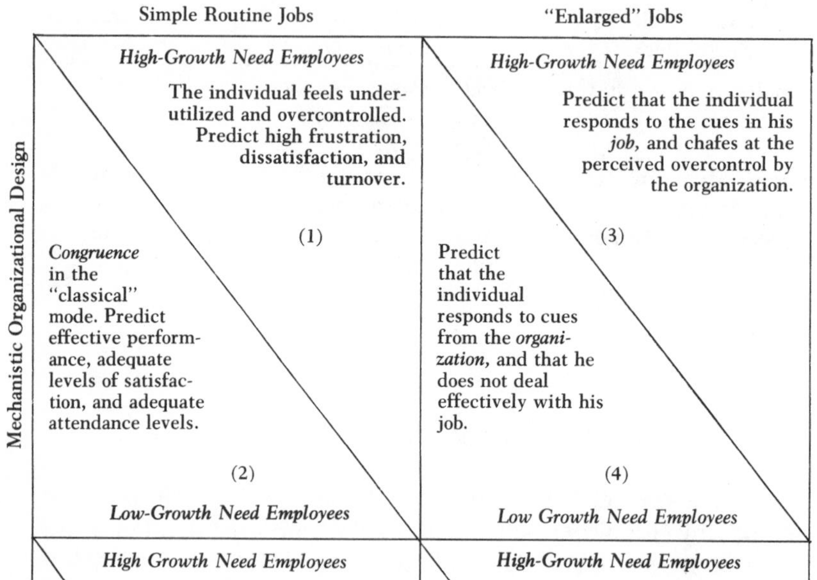

Simple Routine Jobs   "Enlarged" Jobs

Mechanistic Organizational Design

High-Growth Need Employees
The individual feels under-utilized and overcontrolled. Predict high frustration, dissatisfaction, and turnover.
(1)

High-Growth Need Employees
Predict that the individual responds to the cues in his *job,* and chafes at the perceived overcontrol by the organization.
(3)

Congruence in the "classical" mode. Predict effective perform-ance, adequate levels of satisfac-tion, and adequate attendance levels.
(2)
Low-Growth Need Employees

Predict that the individual responds to cues from the *organi-zation,* and that he does not deal effectively with his job.
(4)
Low Growth Need Employees

Organic Organizational Design

High Growth Need Employees
Predict that the individual responds to the cues in the *organization,* and that he chafes at the restrictiveness of his job. Predict he will try and succeed in hav-ing the job changed, or resign.
(5)

High-Growth Need Employees
Congruence in the "flexible" mode. Predict very high quality performance, high satisfaction, good attendance, and low turnover.
(7)

Predict that the individual responds to the cues in his job and that he performs reasonably adequately but that he is con-stantly uneasy and anxious about the per-ceived unpredictability of organizational manage-ment.
(6)
Low-Growth Need Employees

The individual is overwhelmed by organizational and job demands. Predict psychologi-cal withdrawal from the job or overt hos-tility and inadequate job performance. A person killer.
(8)
Low-Growth Need Employees

From Porter, Lawler, and Hackman (1975), p. 301.

those sent by the job itself are quite different. Porter et al. predict that individuals faced with such contradictions will tend to respond to and act in accordance with cues which are congruent with their own need-states. For example, a high growth-need employee faced with a complex job in a mechanistic organization would be expected to respond to cues from the job rather than from the organization.

Pierce, Dunham, and Blackburn (1977) tested the Porter congruency model with a large sample of insurance company employees in a variety of jobs drawn from vertically and horizontally separated work units. Consistent with predictions of the model, employee satisfaction was highest for those individuals who most closely matched the description of cell 5, and lowest for those who matched the description of cell 1 (see Figure 6—2). Findings concerning other cells, however, were often not identical to those predicted by the model.

Nemiroff and Ford (1975, 1976) have formulated another model which considers the fit between the individual, the task, and the structure of the organization. The variables included in their framework are shown in Figure 6—3. Consistent with the Porter model, this model considers whether structure is mechanistic or organic and whether tasks are simple and predictable or complex and uncertain. Also like the Porter model, the Nemiroff and Ford model predicts negative consequences when task characteristics and organization structure are not congruent. However, Nemiroff and Ford consider two individual characteristics—strength of higher-order needs and degree of *bureaucratic orientation.* As used here, bureaucratic orientation is a measure of the extent to which the individual desires a restrictive, formalized structure. Nemiroff and Ford argue that, while strengths of higher-order needs will influence responses to task characteristics, reactions to the overall structure of the organization will largely depend upon bureaucratic orientation. Since an employee could possess any combination of higher-order need strength and degree of bureaucratic orientation,[9] the Nemiroff and Ford model makes some predictions that differ from those of the Porter model. For example, contrary to the predictions of Porter et al., Nemiroff and Ford would not expect employees with strong higher-order needs to react negatively to a mechanis-

[9]*In fact, Nemiroff and Ford report that for two samples of individuals which they considered, measures of higher-order need strength and bureaucratic orientation were not related to each other.*

FIGURE 6—3   Components of the Nemiroff and Ford (1976)
               Model

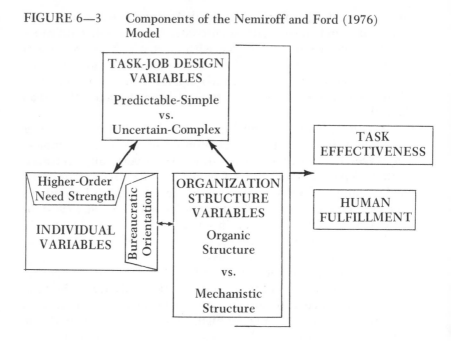

From Nemiroff and Ford (1976).

tic organization structure if those employees were characterized
by high bureaucratic orientation. In general, however, the models
are quite similar in their components and predictions.

Both models must be viewed as tentative. Porter et al.
frankly state that their model is somewhat speculative, and
Nemiroff and Ford present theirs as a guide to future research.
The findings of Pierce et al. suggest that the fit of task to organi-
zation design to employee need strength is important but may be
more complex than was previously assumed. The models seem to
be logical, however, and rest upon theoretically sound bases.
Taken together, they suggest that before job redesign is under-
taken, a careful analysis of the characteristics of the organization
must be conducted. In particular, the models indicate that job
enrichment attempts may meet with limited success in firms
characterized by a mechanistic structure. Such a structure would
be likely to prevent adequate implementation of the job enrich-

ment effort, continually exert pressures to reduce job size, and cause employees to receive conflicting cues concerning appropriate behavior.

TECHNOLOGY

We've now seen that there is both theory and empirical evidence suggesting that the design of an organization influences the effectiveness of particular job redesign efforts. We noted earlier in this chapter that Woodward (1965) found that optimal organization design is a function of technology. In Chapter 4 we pointed out that certain technological constraints might make it difficult to go beyond given limits in enriching a job. Thus, it seems reasonable to expect that the nature of an organization's technology may influence the degree to which it would be feasible or desirable to redesign jobs.

As used here, *technology* refers to the way the organization transforms materials and other inputs into outputs. One popular technological categorization scheme was developed by Thompson (1967). He classified technology into three types, described briefly by Rousseau (1977) as follows:

(1) Long-linked or serially interdependent technologies: Analogous to the mass-production assembly line where tasks must be performed according to a prescribed order. The long-linked technology is based on the predictability of cause-effect relationships with production methods producing predictable changes in raw materials. A high degree of structuring of jobs and work processes characterizes long-linked technologies.

(2) Mediating technologies: Operate through standardized processes, sorting inputs or clients into groups for application of prescribed procedures based on categorization. Such units are characterized by the choice among a variety of processes, each suited to a particular segment of the inputs to a unit, such as product engineering firms, banks, and insurance claims units.

(3) Intensive or custom technologies: Customized ap-

plication of a variety of techniques to an input with the selection of appropriate methods based on feedback from the object. Low cause-effect knowledge exists and this discretionary behavior is required to refine the treatment of inputs as work progresses. Such units are characterized by few standardized procedures and a predominance of problem-solving activity, for example, research and development units and hospitals (pp. 24–25).

These technological types differ in the degree to which the transformation of inputs into outputs is clear to employees, and hence, in the amount of discretion employees may exercise in their work. It might be expected, then, that perceived levels of the task attributes discussed in Chapter 4 would vary as a function of technology. Rousseau (1977) studied nineteen units representing distinct production processes in thirteen organizations. She found that perceived levels of skill variety, task identity, task significance, autonomy, feedback from agents, and dealing with others all varied significantly as a function of technological type. For example, average levels of each of these task attributes were lower in the long-linked, assembly-line organizations than in others.[10] Related findings are reported by Pierce and Dunham (in press). They found that insurance employees' perceptions of technology and of task dimensions actually converged: that is, the employees' responses to questions about the characteristics of their jobs and about the nature of the technology in their units were so closely interrelated that they seemed to be measuring the same things. While such results could indicate measurement problems, they strongly suggest that technology and task design are intimately related.

Such findings demonstrate that the two models of task–organization design fit presented earlier in this chapter may have to be expanded to incorporate technology. In fact, Schuler (1977) has argued that there must be a three-way fit between the technology of the organization, the task, and the organization's structure. In particular, he reasoned that an improper fit between these three factors would result in role conflict and role ambiguity. *Role conflict* refers to the receipt of conflicting mes-

[10]*The situation of units with mediating technologies is complicated. While Rousseau (1977) found such units to be characterized by high perceived levels of the core task dimensions, they are often highly structured. As such, the Porter and Nemiroff and Ford models would suggest that they would not be hospitable to enriched jobs. This issue clearly deserves additional study.*

TABLE 6—4   Sample Items to Assess Role Conflict and Ambiguity

Role Conflict:
I receive incompatible requests from two or more people.
I do things that are apt to be accepted by one person and not by others.
I have to buck a rule or policy in order to carry out an assignment.

Role Ambiguity (reverse-scored):
I know what my responsibilities are.
I feel certain about how much authority I have on the job.
I have clear, planned goals and objectives for my job.

From Rizzo, House, and Lirtzman (1970).

sages concerning the sorts of behaviors expected of an individual in his or her role; *role ambiguity* to a lack of clarity concerning role expectations and uncertainty about the outcomes of performing that role.[11] An employee faced with multiple conflicting cues from the job, the organization design, and the technology of the organization would no doubt experience such role stresses.

One widely used scale to measure levels of role conflict and role ambiguity was developed by Rizzo, House, and Lirtzman (1970).[12] Sample items from that scale are presented in Table 6—4. Each of these role stresses is related to a variety of negative consequences, including tension, turnover, job dissatisfaction, anxiety, and low performance.[13]

As a partial test of his arguments, Schuler (1977) surveyed employees of the engineering division of a large public utility. Since he saw the technology of this organization as being highly complex, Schuler argued that a combination of enriched task and organic structure would provide a congruent fit with the technology, while any other combination of task and organization structure type would be incongruent. Consistent with his arguments, Schuler found role ambiguity to be lowest in the congruent task-organization-technology combination. On the other hand, role conflict turned out to be lower for one of the incongruent combinations than for the congruent match.

As with the models presented earlier in this chapter, it should be noted that Schuler's model, while logically based, is

[11]*For discussions of role theory, see Katz and Kahn (1966); Lichtman and Hunt (1971); and VanSell, Brief, and Schuler (1977).*
[12]*For an assessment of this scale, see Schuler, Aldag, and Brief (1977).*
[13]*For example, see Gross, Mason, and McEachern (1958); Kahn, Wolfe, Quinn, Snoeck, and Rosenthal (1964); House and Rizzo (1972); and Schuler, Aldag, and Brief (1977).*

meant more as a guide for future research than as a final state-
ment concerning this issue. Consequently, while it highlights the
need to focus on a particular set of apparently relevant variables,
much more work is needed before it can be used to make solid
prescriptions for task design.

THE SUBUNIT

To this point we have considered the need to fit the task to
the structure and technology of the organization, as well as to the
desires of the individual. It would be simplistic, however, to
think of organizations as homogeneous in terms of their structure
or technology. For example, Hall (1962) has shown in a sample of
ten organizations that a number of dimensions—including
specialization, impersonality of relationships, emphasis on rules,
and clarity of authority relationships—differed significantly
across both hierarchical levels and departments within organiza-
tions. Thus, it is misleading to think of a firm as uniformly
mechanistic or organic. Further, consideration of only the nature
of the technology of the workflow may be misleading. Hickson,
Pugh, and Pheysey (1969) have broken down the overall concept
of technology into three components: *operations technology* refers
to the techniques used in the workflow activities of the organiza-
tion; *materials technology* refers to the materials used in the
workflow; and *knowledge technology* refers to the knowledge sys-
tem used in the workflow. Hickson et al. argue that as firms
increase in size, the pervasiveness of the impact of operations
technology decreases. Consequently, in large firms, the nature of
the operations technology may not be especially relevant to many
jobs. For example, an automobile manufacturing firm has many
subunits (such as research and development and advertising)
which don't employ a long-linked technology.

What the work of Hall and of Hickson et al. suggests is that,
even if the models of technology-structure-task-individual fit
which have been considered in this chapter are shown to be valid,
some sections of an organization may differ markedly from
others, in terms of both structural characteristics and the rele-
vance of predominant operations technology. Thus, even in a
predominantly mechanistic firm characterized by long-linked

operations technology, many subunits may possess characteristics which would be favorable to enrichment efforts. This suggests that the nature of the particular subunit being considered for job redesign, rather than simply of the overall organization, should be evaluated prior to redesign attempts.

SUMMARY

The material reviewed in this chapter provides compelling evidence that task redesign cannot be carried out without consideration of the context of target jobs. In particular, it appears that an organization's design and technology may exert pressures which influence both the nature of jobs and their effectiveness. While theory and research in this area are in early stages of development, the evidence available suggests that job enrichment is likely to meet with difficulties in cases where the design of the organizational subunit is mechanistic, or the technology of the organization is long-linked. Further, evidence indicates that it is important to consider the fit of individual need strength not only to the job but also to the design of the organizational subunit.

Again, it must be reemphasized that the whole question of this need for a fit between the individual, the task, and the organization's design and technology has rarely been asked, let alone adequately answered. This chapter has considered evidence which should bolster the confidence of individuals about to undertake job enrichment efforts in organic organizational units with mediating or intensive technologies. However, the research evidence is certainly not strong enough to justify abandonment of consideration of such efforts in other sorts of firms.

REFERENCES

Aldag, R. J., and Storey, R. G. Environmental uncertainty: Comments on objective and perceptual indices. *Proceedings of the 35th Annual Meeting of the Academy of Management*, 35, 1975, 203–5.

Argyris, C. *Integrating the Individual and the Organization.* New York: Wiley, 1964.

Burns, T., and Stalker, G. M. *The Management of Innovation.* London: Tavistock, 1961.

Chandler, A. *Strategy and Structure: Chapters in the History of Industrial Enterprise.* Cambridge: M.I.T. Press, 1962.

Filley, A. The parable of the traffic light: Uses and misuses of rules. *MSU Business Topics, 24,* 1976, 57-59.

Gross, N., Mason, W. S., and McEachern, A. W. *Explorations in Role Analysis.* New York: Wiley, 1958.

Guion, R. M. A note on organizational climate. *Organizational Behavior and Human Performance, 9,* 1973, 120-25.

Hall, R. H. Intraorganizational structural variation: Application of the bureaucratic model. *Administrative Science Quarterly, 7,* 1962, 295-308.

Hellriegel, D., and Slocum, J. W., Jr. Organizational climate: Measures, research and contingencies. *Academy of Management Journal, 17,* 1974, 255-80.

Hickson, D. J., Pugh, D. S., and Pheysey, D. C. Operations technology and organization structure: An empirical reappraisal. *Administrative Science Quarterly, 14,* 1969, 378-97.

House, R. J., and Rizzo, J. R. Role conflict and ambiguity as critical variables in a model of organizational behavior. *Organizational Behavior and Human Performance, 7,* 1972, 467-505.

Hunt, R. G. Technology and organization. *Academy of Management Journal, 13,* 1970, 235-52.

James, L. R., and Jones, A. P. Organization climate: A review of theory and research. *Psychological Bulletin, 81,* 1974, 1096-1112.

Johannesson, R. E. Job satisfaction and perceptually measured organization climate: Redundancy and confusion. In *New Developments in Management and Organization Theory,* ed. by M. W. Frey. Proceedings of the Eighth Annual Conference, Eastern Academy of Management, 1971, 27-37.

———— Some problems in the measurement of organization climate. *Organizational Behavior and Human Performance, 10,* 1973, 118-45.

Kahn, R., Wolfe, D., Quinn, R., Snoeck, J., and Rosenthal, R. *Organizational Stress: Studies in Role Conflict and Ambiguity.* New York: Wiley, 1964.

Kast, F. E., and Rosenzweig, J. E. *Contingency Views of Organization and Management.* Chicago: Science Research Associates, 1973.

Katz, D., and Kahn, R. L. *The Social Psychology of Organizations.* New York: Wiley, 1966.

Khandwalla, P. N. Mass output orientation of operations technology and organizational structure. *Administrative Science Quarterly, 19,* 1974, 74–97.

Lawrence, P. R., and Lorsch, J. W. *Organization and Environment.* Homewood, Ill.: Irwin, 1969.

Leavitt, H. J. Unhuman organizations. *Harvard Business Review, 40,* 1962, 90–98.

Lichtman, C. M., and Hunt, R. G. Personality and organization theory: A review of some conceptual literature. *Psychological Bulletin, 76,* 1971, 271–94.

March, J. G., and Simon, H. A. *Organizations.* New York: Wiley, 1958.

Morse, J. J. Organizational characteristics and individual motivation. In *Studies in Organization Design,* ed. by P. R. Lawrence and J. W. Lorsch. Homewood, Ill.: Irwin, 1970.

Nemiroff, P. M., and Ford, D. L., Jr. Task effectiveness and human fulfillment in organizations: A review and development of a conceptual contingency model. *Academy of Management Review, 1(4),* 1976, 69–82.

Perrow, C. A framework for the comparative analysis of organizations. *American Sociological Review, 32,* 1967, 194–208.

Perrow, C. *Organizational Analysis: A Sociological View.* Belmont, Calif.: Wadsworth, 1970.

Pierce, J. L., and Dunham, R. B. An empirical demonstration of the convergence of common macro and micro organization measures. *Academy of Management Journal,* in press.

Pierce, J. L., Dunham, R. B., and Blackburn, R. S. Organization structure, job design and growth need strength: A test of a congruency model. Working paper, University of Minnesota—Duluth, 1977.

Porter, L. W., Lawler, E. E. III, and Hackman, J. R. *Behavior in Organizations.* New York: McGraw-Hill, 1975.

Rizzo, J. R., House, R. J., and Lirtzman, S. I. Role conflict and ambiguity in complex organizations. *Administrative Science Quarterly, 15,* 1970, 150–63.

Rousseau, D. M. Technological differences in job characteristics, employee satisfaction, and motivation: A synthesis of job design research and sociotechnical systems theory. *Organizational Behavior and Human Performance, 19,* 1977, 18–42.

Schuler, R. S. Role conflict and ambiguity as a function of the task-structure-technology interaction. *Organizational Behavior and Human Performance, 20,* 1977, 60–74.

Schuler, R. S., Aldag, R. J., and Brief, A. P. Role conflict and ambiguity: A scale analysis. *Organizational Behavior and Human Performance, 20,* 1977, 111–28.

Stinchcombe, A. L. Bureaucratic and craft administration of production: A comparative study. *Administrative Science Quarterly, 4,* 1959, 168–87.

Tagiuri, R. The concept of organization climate. In *Organizational Climate: Explorations of a Concept,* ed. by R. Tagiuri and G. Litwin. Boston: Division of Research, Graduate School of Business, Harvard University, 1969.

Thompson, J. D. *Organizations in Action.* New York: McGraw-Hill, 1967.

Tosi, H., Aldag, R. J., and Storey, R. G. On the measurement of the environment: An assessment of the Lawrence and Lorsch Environmental Uncertainty subscales. *Administrative Science Quarterly, 18,* 1973, 27–36.

Udy, S. *Organization of Work: A Comparative Analysis of Production Among Non-Industrial Peoples.* New Haven: Human Relations Area File Press, 1959.

———. Administrative rationality, social setting, and organizational development. In *New Perspectives in Organization Research,* ed. by W. W. Cooper, H. J. Leavitt, and M. W. Shelley II. New York: Wiley, 1964.

VanSell, M., Brief, A. P., and Schuler, R. S. Role conflict and role ambiguity: A review and synthesis of the literature. Working paper, University of Iowa, 1977.

Woodward, J. *Industrial Organization: Theory and Practice.* London: Oxford University Press, 1965.

The Changing Role of the Worker

7

WORKING ENVIRONMENT ACT: SECTION 12

1. General Requirements
Production methods, work organization, working hours (e.g., shift work and schedules) and payment systems shall be so designed as to avoid harmful physiological or psychological effects on employees, including any negative influence on the alertness necessary for reasons of safety.

Employees shall be afforded opportunities for personal development and the maintenance and development of their skills.

2. Job Design
Full account shall be taken of the need for employee self-determination and maintenance of skills in the planning of work and design of jobs.

Monotonous, repetitive work and machine or assembly line work that does not permit alteration of pace shall be avoided.

Jobs shall be so designed as to allow some possibility for variation, for contact with other workers, for interdependence between their constituent elements, and for information and feedback to the employees concerning production requirements and performance.

3. Planning and Control Systems
Employees or their representatives shall be kept informed about planning and control systems, including any changes in such systems. They shall be given the necessary training to understand the systems adopted and shall have the right to influence their design . . . .

The requirements listed above read like the fantasies of a discontented employee. Along with concern for employee health and safety, they emphasize personal development and self-determination. The need for variety in work, for feedback, and for the opportunity to participate in job design are stressed. In fact, these requirements represent not idle dreams but the hard reality of a Working Environment Act placed before the Norwegian Parliament in December of 1976.[1] That act is just one reflection of a growing movement, in Europe and elsewhere, toward increased worker participation in what have traditionally been viewed as managerial functions.

The term *worker participation* is often used as a catch-all to cover employee participation at any one of a variety of content levels. As categorized by Koch and Fox (1977), worker participation may take place at one or more of three decision content-levels, *institutional, managerial,* and *technical.* As shown in Figure 7—1, examples of formal worker participation in institutional, managerial, and technical decisions would be worker representatives on boards of directors, in workers' councils, and in trade unions. Job enrichment, as it has been considered in previous chapters, is viewed by Koch and Fox as an informal means of participation in technical decisions.

While worker participation in managerial and institutional decisions in the United States is still very limited, U.S. multinational firms are already feeling the influence abroad of laws relating to worker involvement. For example, the German Codetermination Act of 1976 requires that most incorporated companies with more than two thousand employees have equal representation of employees and shareholders on the board of supervisors, a body akin to our board of directors.[2] Thirty-three

---

[1] *For a discussion of this act, see Gustavsen (1977).*
[2] *For fuller discussions of codetermination, see Agthe (1977); Garson (1977); Kühne (1976); Prasad (1977); and* Nation's Business *(1976).*

FIGURE 7—1   Content Levels and Forms of Worker Participation

Content Levels	Forms of Participation	
	[a]Formal Shared Power	[b]Informal Participation
Institutional (Higher-Level Decisions): Overall organizational policy & strategy.	A Worker Representatives on Boards of Directors Worker Cooperatives	D Advisory Influence of Hospital Physicians and Faculty Senates
Managerial (Mid-Level Decisions): Control/administration of technical suborganization.	B Workers' Councils Worker Cooperatives Trade Unions	E Semi-autonomous Units—worker roles encompass department operation, staffing levels, determination of rewards (e.g., Scanlon Plans)
Technical (Job-Level Decisions): Material/resource processing and service delivery	C Trade Unions	F Job restructuring/enrichment, MBO, Likert's System IV Management

[a]Rational-legal basis of authority or influence.
[b]Authority based on competence or expertise in a specialized knowledge area: a function of tacit understandings and/or efforts to improve human resource utilization through innovations in the management subsystem.
From Koch and Fox (1977).

U.S. companies, employing almost two hundred thousand individuals, are subject to this new law. In addition, there is reason to believe that worker participation at all decision levels will continue to grow in Europe and will increasingly influence U.S. multinational firms. For example, the Commission of European Communities has recently adopted a codetermination model. Companies doing business in more than one European country will have the option under the European Company Law to become a "European company" rather than registering under existing national laws.[3] The law aims at encouraging transnational business and worker participation, and shielding firms from the disrupting influences of unpredictable changes in national policies.[4] Under the law, the company supervisory board will be composed of one-third shareholders' representatives, one-third employees' representatives, and one-third representatives of "general interests." In addition, a system of *works councils*—employee groups that consult with management on such issues as production and working conditions—is required by the law. U.S. subsidiaries could elect this option. Further, as pointed out by Garson (1977), firms operating in Italy, France, Spain, and other European countries lacking codetermination could, by incorporating as European companies, bring the codetermination model into those countries and serve as indigenous role models.

On the other hand, there are major differences between the United States and Europe in terms of labor market conditions, attitudes toward the appropriate nature of union-management relationships, general economic conditions, labor political strength, dependence upon international markets, class distinctions, and a number of other important factors. Each of those differences argues against the probability of substantially increased worker involvement in managerial and institutional decisions in the United States in the near future.[5] Rather, increases in worker participation are likely to be confined to the sorts of technical decisions which have been the focus of this book.

This chapter will examine how employee participation in technical decisions is changing in the United States and

---

[3]*For discussions of the European Company Law, see Garson (1977) and Kühne (1976).*
[4]*On this point, see Fawcett (1975).*
[5]*For discussions of this issue, see Foy and Gadon (1976); Jenkins (1973); Koch and Fox (1977); and Nation's Business (1976).*

elsewhere. While to this point we have tried to present evidence concerning whether, when, and to what extent job redesign might be desirable and how it could best be implemented, this chapter is primarily devoted to a survey of the current worldwide status of job redesign. Thus, it is largely descriptive rather than prescriptive. Such a descriptive focus is necessary in order to stress the growing reality of pressures for redesign, to indicate some of the alternative approaches which have been taken, and to provide additional clues concerning potentially relevant factors which may affect the success of redesign attempts.

This chapter will first consider the status of job redesign in Sweden, a country which has led the United States in redesign attempts, and will then detail some redesign efforts in this country. Finally, a few additional contingencies concerning job redesign which are brought to light on the basis of worldwide experience will be examined.

THE SITUATION IN SWEDEN

Pressure for job redesign has been evident in Britain, France, West Germany, Belgium, Israel, Peru, and elsewhere.[6] The case of Sweden is highlighted here because of Sweden's relatively extensive experience with the sorts of job redesign at the technical level which have been the focus of this book. Like other Scandinavian countries, Sweden has in recent years seen an increased emphasis on worker participation, reflected both in a number of experiments on job redesign and in legislation.

Sweden's unions are politically influential and have played an active role in lobbying for such legislation and experimentation. Approximately 90 percent of Swedish blue-collar workers are members of unions belonging to the Confederation of Trade Unions (LO), while about 50 percent of white-collar workers belong to unions comprising the Central Organization of Salaried Employees (TCO). Bargaining for each industry occurs at the national level through the Swedish Employers' Federation

[6]For some discussions of the status of worker participation elsewhere, see Aaron (1974); Gustavsen (1977); Jenkins (1973, 1976); Kühne (1976); Mire (1973); Paul, Robertson, and Herzberg (1969); Robinson (1976); and Schregle (1970).

(SAF), with agreements then working down to the local level.[7] The pervasive role of Swedish unions is evident in the listing of Swedish legislation and other developments relevant to worker participation presented in Table 7—1.

As suggested by this listing, Sweden has not relied heavily on legislation to increase employee participation until quite recently, stressing instead the concept of *voluntarism*.[8] Many widely publicized experiments, generally emphasizing the relationship between social and technical subsystems, stressed labor-management cooperation.[9] As one conspicuous example, Volvo constructed an assembly plant at Kalmar, Sweden, using a flexible production system. The showcase plant did away with assembly lines, using instead about twenty-five teams of fifteen to twenty-five persons each. Each team handles a general area, such as electrical wiring or door assembly. While there is still an emphasis on production quotas, the approach allows workers to change jobs or even teams. There is an emphasis upon open communications between workers on the plant floor and the plant manager, as well as upon such extrinsics as saunas for each team, laundry service for work clothes, lounges, and other amenities.

Many other sorts of experiments—involving training, changes in means of compensation, or decentralization—have been attempted. Volkswagen of Sweden instituted work teams in its repair shops and moved from a piecework wage system to one composed of part fixed income and part team productivity premium. Kockums, a diversifying shipbuilding firm, developed in 1969 a completely new product and organization structure in response to a union study. The redesign featured self-managing groups, monthly pay for all employees, group bonuses, and a consultation arrangement involving over 10 percent of all employees. The Skandia Insurance Company undertook in 1968 a decentralization which left top management members working in a bullpen without individual offices. Euroc, a building materials conglomerate, instituted in 1973 a company-wide program for employee education and consultation. Interestingly, Foy and Gadon (1976) note that the concept of flexible working hours, one aspect of participation which is increasingly seen in the United States and Britain, is almost unknown in Sweden.

[7]See Foy and Gadon (1976).
[8]For a discussion of codetermination, voluntarism, and co-optation of the left as alternative models, see Garson (1977).
[9]These examples are taken from Peterson (1976); Foy and Gadon (1976); and Garson (1977).

TABLE 7—1   Relevant Swedish Legislation and Other
                Developments

1906: In return for the right of workers to organize, management was
      given the *right to manage.* The right to manage gave
      management the right to hire and fire employees, to allocate
      work, and to have the final word in any agreements unless they
      were taken to labor court by union or employees.

1946: Works councils became a legal requirement.

1966: The *Development Council for Collaborative Questions* was
      established by the SAF, LO, and TCO for the purpose of
      seeking new avenues to enhancement of worker satisfaction,
      influence, and productivity. The council did relatively little
      until 1969, when results of Norwegian experiments became
      known. The council recommended that experiments in job
      reform be undertaken, and a number of collaboration councils
      were formed to oversee experiments in the private sector, at
      the national government level, and in counties and
      municipalities.* Some firms, such as Volvo, carried out
      experiments independent of such councils.

1970: Olof Palme, the Swedish prime minister, calling for
      improvements in the plant to match those accomplished
      elsewhere in society, stressed the need to change both extrinsic
      and intrinsic factors. "The task of the '70s," he said, "must be
      to give the worker a better surrounding and more say over his
      work at the workplace."

1972: The potency of the right to manage was dampened by a law
      making it difficult to terminate employees after six months.
      The *Rationalization Agreement* stated that changes in production
      methods should be aimed at four equally important areas of
      improvement: productivity, job satisfaction, working
      environment, and job security. Consultation with employees
      was required prior to such changes.

1973: The employee-director law required direct election of
      blue-collar and white-collar representatives to boards of
      companies with over two hundred employees upon union
      demand.

1974: Employee safety representatives were given the right to shut
      down operations believed to be dangerous.

1975: An agreement between the LO and the SAF required
      companies to give works councils full access to financial data.

1977: The *Democracy at Work Act,* eliminating the right to manage,
      came into effect. Employees were given the first right of
      interpretation, with management left in the position of having
      to appeal in labor court.

---

*For a discussion of the councils and experiments, see Peterson (1976).

Success of the experiments has been mixed. For example, Volvo's Kalmar plant cost 10 percent more to build than a conventional facility despite the fact that the land was contributed by the government. Operating costs are higher than in a conventional plant and Kalmar can turn out only sixty thousand cars a year with a double work turn compared to two hundred thousand for a typical U.S. plant and four hundred thousand at General Motors' Lordstown, Ohio, facility. However, quality of output appears to be higher than elsewhere, and absenteeism and turnover have been reduced and are lower than in other area plants. It should be noted, however, that the Kalmar staff was young and carefully chosen and that a tighter labor market could be a partial explanation for the reduced turnover. Furthermore, when a team of six U.S. auto workers went to Sweden to examine a Saab auto engine plant designed much like Kalmar, they were generally unenthusiastic. In particular, one worker noted that jobs in Detroit were "more relaxed" since the workers could daydream on the assembly line. Most of the workers' positive comments related not to intrinsics but to such extrinsics as cleanliness and noise levels. The Kalmar experiment also suggests that short-run evaluations may be inadequate. As one woman working at Kalmar explained, "It was fun at first, but now it has gotten routine."[10]

Other experiments have met with similar mixed results. For instance, the changes at Skandia Insurance Company have resulted in no change in productivity, slightly increased absenteeism, and slight increases in satisfaction and climate perceptions. At Atlas Copco, a manufacturer of air compressors and rock drilling equipment, productivity increased after the assembly line was replaced by work teams. However, while the changes took place in a small department and were expected to be completed in six weeks, they in fact were not begun until eighteen months after the proposal. The experiment was terminated by a new manager when workers began to press for broader participation in decision-making. Some experiments in other firms either failed to be implemented or were never adopted elsewhere within the experimenting organizations. A number of factors, including lack of expertise, uncontrollable developments, and negative reactions of managerial and supervisory personnel, was blamed for such results.

One relevant issue highlighted by such projects is that job

[10]Wall Street Journal, 1977.

redesign efforts cannot be undertaken without careful consideration of the potential impact of the resultant changes on employee compensation. There are at least two reasons for this. First, workers may simply fear that changes will result in reduced pay. Björk (1975) reports that delays at Atlas Copco, noted above, were caused by concerns over possible pay loss. Second, workers may feel that the greater number of required skills and heightened responsibility associated with enriched jobs should justify increases in pay. For instance, Peterson (1976) notes that workers affected by the redesign of the engine assembly operation at the Södertälje plant of Saab-Scandia argued that their new skills benefited the firm in terms of flexibility of assignment and increased productivity and that improved pay packages were thus justified.[11]

One objection to the Swedish experiments is that they have generally failed either to spread out of the experimental sector of the economy or to result in democratization at higher organizational levels.[12] Garson (1977) views such difficulties as among the reasons why Swedish unions began in the early 1970s to press for legislation guaranteeing workers' rights instead of relying on voluntarism. The listing of legal developments in Table 7—1 suggests that Sweden has in fact moved substantially toward the codetermination model mentioned earlier. In response to the newly enacted Democracy at Work Act, Swedish unions are assigning one hundred eighty labor executives to take places on corporate boards and are instituting programs of participation for over twenty thousand other unionists.[13]

DEVELOPMENTS IN THE UNITED STATES

As noted previously, most instances of employee involvement in organizational discussions in the United States occur at the technical level. Exceptions pointed out by Koch and Fox

[11]*In a related vein, Dunham (in press) found that overall job complexity as measured by the Job Diagnostic Survey bears a significant relationship to job evaluation points, a measure of the "value" of the job. Also, Aldag and Brief (1975) reported significant correlations between levels of core task dimensions and manufacturing employees' pay.*
[12]*Garson (1977), p. 67.*
[13]*Ibid., p. 68.*

(1977) include workers' cooperatives in the northwest plywood industry and the custom of participation by hospital physicians and university faculties in the decision processes of their respective institutions.

There have, however, been a few conspicuous examples of job redesign in the United States which are notable.[14] McCormick and Company, a Baltimore producer of spices and other commodities, instituted about thirty years ago a system termed *multiple management*, using employee boards which acted as lower-level versions of the board of directors. Composed of middle managers, the boards can make recommendations in all areas except where wages or questions concerning individuals are concerned. Over a five-year period, one board made over two thousand recommendations, all but six of which were adopted as policy. Along with the fact that the arrangement allows increased influence by middle management, it is viewed as a useful development device. However, since, as one top executive put it, "Charlie McCormick used to say that one out of ten knows how to think," employees at lower hierarchical levels are not involved in decision-making.[15]

When the Spalding Division of the Questor Corporation built its new golf club factory in 1969, management decided to give employees more opportunity for participation. Trust was stressed: time clocks were abolished and straight salary was given to everyone; foremen and formal inspectors were eliminated; workers were given considerable say in changing their work assignments; employee suggestions were encouraged. Spalding claims that the plant's costs are 15 percent below those of comparable plants, and that efficiency, safety, absenteeism, and turnover are all at favorable levels.

Donnelly Mirrors, a small non-union company in Michigan, has since 1952 used a version of the Scanlon Plan, devised in the late 1930s by Joseph Scanlon.[16] Under the Scanlon Plan, management and labor representatives determine a "normal" past period in order to define measures of efficiency. It is agreed

[14]*For a detailed, though perhaps optimistic, discussion of job redesign efforts in the United States, see Jenkins (1973). Some examples in this section are drawn from that source.*

[15]*Jenkins (1973), p. 221.*

[16]*For discussions of the Scanlon Plan, see Lesieur (1958) and Lesieur and Puckett (1969).*

that when performance exceeds a particular level, based on these measures, a percentage of the resulting increased profit is split among all employees. A series of committees is set up to evaluate employee suggestions and those considered valuable are put into effect. In 1968, Donnelly Mirrors went further and replaced traditional work groups with semiautonomous teams. The employees, now all salaried, participate in planning and decision-making, including decisions concerning their own raises. Productivity in the eight months following the changes rose by almost 50 percent compared to the previous eight months.

Jenkins (1973) states that "without doubt the most radical organizational changes made on a practical, operating, day-to-day basis in the United States have taken place at Procter & Gamble, America's twenty-first largest company and well known for its hard-boiled, aggressive management practices" (p. 231). A P&G plant in Lima, Ohio, with about 125 employees was consciously designed to be democratic. According to Charles Krone, head of organizational development at P&G's Cincinnati headquarters, "technology—the location of instruments, for example—was designed to stimulate relationships between people, to bring about autonomous group behavior, and to allow people to affect their own environment."[17] Further, while there might be sixteen to twenty job classifications at a conventional plant, there are none at Lima. All employees (members of "the community" in Krone's words)—while they can't necessarily do every job—continually learn new skills. They choose the direction of their own development subject to certain constraints, such as that everyone must take some responsibility for day-to-day operations. Members of the community hire and fire, work out pay scales, and interact with suppliers, corporate headquarters specialists, outside consultants, and other members of the plant environment. Overall costs at the plant are reportedly about 50 percent of those of a conventional plant, while quality is considered virtually perfect. The principles upon which the plant was established have been successful enough that they are being employed both in other new P&G plants and in established operations.

At General Foods, a planning group took a *total systems approach* when planning the Topeka, Kansas, pet food plant. The nature of the plant's operations was analyzed in terms of probable

[17]*Jenkins (1973), p. 231.*

impacts on employee self-esteem, autonomy, feelings of achievement, and so on. As a result, work teams—each with team leaders but without direct supervisors—were set up. Employees learned all jobs on their teams. Progress in learning was judged by fellow team members, with pay increases based upon that progress. Status symbols were de-emphasized, time clocks were eliminated, and written statements concerning expected behavior were kept to a minimum. About 80 percent of employees felt that the quality of their working life had improved. After eighteen months, the overhead rate was 33 percent lower than in the old plant, absenteeism was 9 percent below the industry norm, and turnover was well below average.[18] Walton (1975) points out, however, that despite the success of the Topeka plant and despite top management attempts to spread the Topeka innovations to other parts of General Foods, little diffusion resulted. This case also illustrates the difficulties involved in evaluating such experiments. As noted by Walton:

> The Topeka plant was new, was located in a favorable labor market, required few workers, and was geographically separate from headquarters and other existing facilities of GF. Since it was a new plant with a new work force, no union agreement was required to establish the new work structure. Many of these conditions, of course, did not exist elsewhere in GF, and many managers asked, "Is work restructuring possible in other situations—for example, in a large, unionized plant?" (p. 13).

These examples demonstrate that some U.S. firms have attempted to enrich employees' jobs and have, in at least a few cases, set up formal mechanisms to encourage employee inputs into top-level decision-making. However, the sorts of developments seen in Europe, where labor has a strong voice in the actual running of the company, are still rare in the United States. As in the Swedish experiments, the success of U.S. redesign attempts is generally difficult to evaluate because of a variety of confounding factors. In at least some cases, the attempts appear to have been successful from the points of view of both employees and management. In certain others, failures could be traced to errors of implementation rather than to innate flaws in design.

[18]*Walton (1975), p. 7.*

Clearly though, some situations appear to be markedly better suited to job redesign than others. Such findings sharply reinforce the contentions of this book that job redesign is not uniformly desirable in all situations and that it must be carefully implemented even in favorable situations.

LESSONS OF WORLD EXPERIENCE

A number of relevant factors to be considered before and during redesign have been noted in previous chapters. The worldwide experience with job redesign provides a number of clues concerning additional factors which may influence the success of such attempts.

Top management support. As with the implementation of any other sort of program, sustained top management support and recognition of that support by others in the firm are crucial to the success of job redesign. Walton (1975) cites cases in Great Britain and Norway in which inconsistent top management behavior crippled diffusion efforts. Peterson (1976), in his review of Swedish experiments, echoes this point, stating that Volvo's position as an international leader in job redesign experiments is largely due to the strong support and encouragement provided by the managing director, Pehr Gyllenhammer.

Compatibility of technology. Chapter 6 pointed out that there is reason to believe that certain technologies may better "fit" job redesign than others. It may also be the case that some technologies are simply harder to change than others. Peterson (1976), writing of Swedish experiments in job redesign, notes that, "in some cases . . . the production process itself has limited experimentation. There was general agreement that it is easier to redesign process technology than either mass or small-batch technology. Changing process technology is favored because tasks are less tied to a given work situation and the worker has a variety of skills" (p. 17).

Ease of adoption and diffusion. Chapter 4 discussed ways to implement a job redesign intervention. Many factors influence whether a particular intervention might be attempted and whether initial experimental efforts will be adopted on a large scale. For example, the literature on determinants of the adoption rate for innovations suggests that the following factors are important:

1. Relative advantage: The extent to which the innovation can be shown to provide net social and financial benefits.

2. Communicability: The degree to which the innovation is easily explainable.

3. Compatibility: The extent to which the innovation is seen as congruent with existing norms, values, and structures.

4. Pervasiveness: The degree to which a number of aspects of the system are affected by the innovation.

5. Reversibility: The ability to adopt the innovation on an experimental basis and reverse it without serious consequences.

6. Number of gatekeepers: The number of approval channels that must be satisfied before an innovation can be adopted.[19]

High relative advantage, communicability, compatibility, and reversibility, and low pervasiveness and number of gatekeepers will enhance the diffusion of the job redesign innovation. As Walton (1975) points out, many of these desirable conditions are difficult to achieve in the case of job redesign. Nevertheless, they represent variables that should be consciously considered prior to the redesign attempt in order to enhance the probability of success.

Several other factors influencing job redesign success are suggested by the results of previous redesign attempts. There is reason to believe that redesign may be easier in a small company, with relatively great flexibility, than in large firms.[20] Further, it is simpler to build job reforms into the design of a new plant than to try to change an old plant with its existing technology, historical interaction patterns and authority structure, and entrenched attitudes. Finally, such factors as continuity of key personnel, employee competencies, project length, and degree of interdependency of jobs will all play a part in the feasibility of successful job redesign.

---

[19]*This specific listing is taken from Walton (1975), p. 20. His article discusses how each of these factors were relevant in explaining why, despite their apparent success, several small-scale job redesign attempts in a number of firms were not widely adopted elsewhere in the firms.*
[20]*See Foy and Gadon (1976).*

SUMMARY

This chapter has provided a summary of the current status of job redesign, focusing on the specific cases of Sweden and the United States. The evidence suggests that there is a trend, especially in Europe, toward a codetermination model, with employees heavily involved in high-level decision-making. While U.S. multinational firms will increasingly have to deal with the reality of codetermination, job redesign in the United States is likely to continue to take place largely at the technical level.

Experimental job redesigns in Sweden and the United States have brought to light additional factors which appear to influence the success of redesign attempts. While pressures for job redesign are a real and growing force, some situations are more suitable than others for redesign attempts and careful implementation of such attempts is crucial. Thus we return to the central theme of this book: successful job redesign requires a thorough, multiple-stage procedure that considers all potentially relevant contingencies.

REFERENCES

Aaron, B. Israel. In *Industry's Democratic Revolution,* ed. by C. Levinson. London: Allen & Unwin, 1974.

Agthe, K. E. Mitbestimmung: Report on a social experiment. *Business Horizons, 20,* 1977, 5-14.

Aldag, R. J., and Brief, A. P. Impact of interactions of task characteristics and employee needs, traits, and abilities. *Proceedings of the Sixth Annual Midwest AIDS Conference,* 1975, 240-42.

Björk, L. An experiment in work satisfaction. *Scientific American, 229,* 1975, 17-23.

Dunham, R. B. Perceived job design, manpower requirements, and job value. *Journal of Applied Psychology,* in press.

Fawcett, E. European companies. *European Community, 188,* 1975, 3-6.

Foy, N., and Gadon, H. Worker participation: Contrasts in three countries. *Harvard Business Review, 54,* 1976, 71-83.

Garson, G. D. The codetermination model of workers' participation: Where is it leading? *Sloan Management Review, 19,* 1977, 63–78.

Gustavsen, G. A legislative approach to job reform in Norway. *International Labor Review, 115,* 1977, 263–76.

Jenkins, D. *Job Power: Blue and White Collar Democracy.* Garden City, N.Y.: Doubleday, 1973.

————. Industrial democracy: It catches on faster in Europe than in U.S. *New York Times,* May 13, 1976.

Koch, J. L., and Fox, C. L. The influence of societal, institutional, and organizational forces on the scope of worker participation in the United States. Working paper, University of Oregon, 1977.

Kühne, R. J. Co-determination: A statutory re-structuring of the organization. *Columbia Journal of World Business, 11,* 1976, 17–25.

Lesieur, F. G. *The Scanlon Plan.* Cambridge, Mass.: M.I.T. Press, 1958.

Lesieur, F. G., and Puckett, E. S. The Scanlon Plan has proved itself. *Harvard Business Review, 47,* 1969, 109–18.

Mire, J. European workers' participation in management. *Monthly Labor Review, 96,* 1973, 9–15.

Nation's Business. Workers on your board of directors? February 1976, 52–54.

Paul, W. J., Jr., Robertson, K. B., and Herzberg, F. Job enrichment pays off. *Harvard Business Review, 47,* 1969, 61–78.

Peterson, R. B. Swedish experiments in job reform. *Business Horizons, 19,* June 1976, 13–22.

Prasad, S. B. The growth of co-determination. *Business Horizons, 20,* 1977, 23–29.

Robinson, R. D. The Peruvian experiment. Research report, Massachusetts Institute of Technology, April 1976.

Schregle, J. Forms of participation in management. *Industrial Relations, 9,* 1970, 117–22.

Wall Street Journal. Battling boredom: Auto plant in Sweden scores some success with worker teams. March 1, 1977.

Walton, R. E. The diffusion of new work structures: Explaining why success didn't take. *Organizational Dynamics, 3,* Winter 1975, 3–22.

Summary

8

The primary purpose of this book has been to provide a systematic, practical, research-based approach to job design. Steps needed to assess the probable success of redesign efforts and stages in the redesign process have been detailed. Where possible, specific instruments which managers can confidently use to make necessary measurements have been outlined. Above all, the book attempts to highlight important contingencies.

Employees consciously and rationally choose the direction in which they apply their efforts, as well as the amount and duration of those efforts. Such choices are based upon employees' beliefs about which behaviors will lead to outcomes capable of satisfying their existence, relatedness, or growth needs. Thus, in order to influence employee behavior, the manager must gain control over those work-derived outcomes that the employee values.

The array of outcomes which the employee may value is large, including, for instance, money, promotions, social reinforcements from co-workers and superiors, status, challenging and responsible work, autonomy, and feelings of meaningfulness and accomplishment. These outcomes can be classified as intrinsic or extrinsic; that is, derived from the work itself, or from such external sources as pay, benefits, or work environment. Intrinsic motivation is positively associated with job satisfaction. In addition, if employees perceive job performance as the vehicle for acquiring such intrinsic outcomes, then intrinsic motivation will also be positively associated with job performance. Thus, employees who occupy jobs designed to provide such intrinsic rewards contingent upon performance should experience relatively high levels of job satisfaction and should perform at relatively high levels.

But employees differ both in the ways they perceive their tasks and in their responses to such perceptions. Because individuals may see the same objective task characteristics differently, job activities which to an outside observer seem to offer high levels of variety, autonomy, and other core task dimensions may be viewed as routine and constraining by the employee. Thus it is necessary to examine the relationships between job activities and incumbents' perceptions of task attributes. Further, since individuals differ in their desires for task attributes, it is also necessary to assess these desires. While urbanization indices, general work values, age, sex, and other variables have sometimes been used as indices of desires for enriched jobs, direct assessment of the strength of higher-order needs is a more promising method of measuring readiness for job redesign. The existence of individual differences in perceptions also requires that employees' perceptions of current levels of task dimensions and satisfaction with extrinsic outcomes be measured.

Task design and the design of the organizational subunit in which the task is housed are also clearly linked. Job redesign is most likely to result in favorable outcomes for the employee and the organization when such redesign meshes with the structure and technology of the subunit. In particular, job enrichment will probably meet with problems when the structure of the subunit is mechanistic or technology is long-linked. Conversely, units characterized by organic structure and intensive technology should be hospitable to enrichment attempts.

In sum, a number of factors relating to job incumbents, the nature of target jobs, characteristics of the organizational reward system, and the structural and technological environment of the target jobs must be assessed before job redesign is undertaken. A family of jobs should be considered for redesign if each of the following conditions is met:

> 1. The job incumbents perceive their jobs as deficient in terms of such core task dimensions as variety, autonomy, task identity, task significance, or feedback.

2. Levels of extrinsic outcomes are considered adequate by job incumbents.

3. The current technology and structure of the subunit in which the tasks are housed are hospitable to enriched jobs and do not prohibit redesign because of excessive costs of new capital investment.

4. The current and potential employees in the target jobs view high levels of core task dimensions as positively valent.

If the above conditions are met, a job redesign task force composed of management and labor representatives should proceed through the following five steps:

1. Identification of the actual activities which currently comprise the family of jobs;

2. Identification of the specific relationships between those activities and the job incumbents' perceptions of salient task attributes (e.g., variety, autonomy, task identity, task significance, and feedback);

3. Specification of a detailed job redesign intervention derived from study of the job activities–task attributes linkages thus detected.

4. Evaluation of the proposed intervention through experiments in selected parts of the organization;

5. If evaluation is favorable, diffusion of the intervention throughout the family of jobs.

Pressures to improve the lot of the worker are increasing in the U.S. and elsewhere. In Europe, one consequence of such pressures has been the widespread adoption of codetermination, with workers participating in managerial- and institutional-level decisions. While U.S. multinational firms will have to recognize and adjust to the reality of codetermination, it is likely that calls for increased worker participation in the United States will be directed more toward the sort of job redesign which has been the subject of this book. Whether, and how, firms should respond to such calls will depend on the kinds of considerations detailed above. Firms faced with demands for change should not turn to job enrichment as a panacea, for some individuals do not want enriched jobs and some situations will not permit successful job enrichment. Even if job enrichment seems to be the appropriate remedy for worker discontent, undue haste in implementation is likely to lead to poor results. Consequently, we hope this book will assist managers in making thoughtful job redesign decisions which will be responsive to the needs of employees without undermining the goals of the organization.

NAME INDEX

Aaron, B., 131
Agthe, K. E., 128
Aldag, R. J., 17, 21, 49, 59, 85, 86, 88,
    89, 92, 94, 112, 121, 135
Alderfer, C. P., 10-11, 64, 87
Allenspach, H., 68
Andersson, B., 2
Archer, W. B., 66
Argyris, C., 40, 64, 109, 110, 111
Armenakis, A. A., 68
Ash, P., 92

Babbage, C., 38
Bamforth, K. W., 42, 46
Bandura, A., 28
Barrett, R. S., 84
Baum, S. J., 68
Beckhard, R., 64
Beer, M., 64
Behling, O., 21
Bell, D., 40, 49, 60
Bennis, W. G., 64
Berger, C. J., 29
Biggane, J. F., 42
Biglan, A., 21
Blackburn, R. S., 117, 118
Blauner, R., 40
Blood, M. R., 41, 42, 83, 84, 85, 86
Bluestone, I., 3
Brewer, E., 2
Bridwell, L., 10
Brief, A. P., 17, 21, 49, 59, 85, 86, 88,
    89, 92, 94, 121, 135
Brown, W., 46
Bugental, D., 89
Burns, T., 2, 108, 109, 114

Campbell, D. T., 69
Campbell, J. P., 2, 44, 18
Canter, R. R., 40, 42
Carlson, S., 2
Caro, F. G., 69
Cartledge, N., 62
Centers, R., 89
Chandler, A., 114
Cherns, A. B., 36
Collins, B. E., 25
Conant, E. H., 42, 84
Converse, P., 89
Cook, T. D., 69
Cummings, L. L., 23, 27, 29, 49, 59

Davis, J. A., 12, 16
Davis, L. E., 3, 36, 40, 42
DeCharms, R., 21
Deci, E. L., 21
DeVries, D. L., 28
Doyle, F. P., 45
Drucker, P. F., 1
Dubin, R., 2, 13, 36
Dunham, R. B., 49, 59, 99, 100,
    117, 120, 135
Dunnette, M. D., 12, 18, 23, 44

Elliott, J. D., 42
Evans, M. G., 68
Ewen, R. B., 44

Fawcett, E., 130
Fein, M., 3, 45
Ferguson, D. A., 97
Field, H. S., 68
Filley, A., 3, 111
Fleishman, E. A., 2
Ford, D. L., Jr., 117, 118
Ford, R. N., 45
Fox, C. L., 128, 130, 135
Foy, N., 130, 132, 140
Frank, L. L., 49, 59

Gadon, H., 130, 132, 140
Galitz, W. O., 42
Garrett, J. B., 86
Garson, G. D., 128, 130, 132, 135
Gellerman, S. W., 12
George, C. S., 36, 38
Ghiselli, E. E., 2
Gilbreth, F. B., 39, 71
Gilbreth, L., 71
Gillespie, D. F., 24
Gillespie, J. J., 40
Golembiewski, R. T., 41, 68
Goodale, J. G., 85, 86
Gooding, J., 43, 44
Graen, G., 18, 44
Green, C., 12
Gross, N., 121
Guest, R. H., 40, 42
Guetzkow, H. A., 25
Guion, R. M., 23, 108
Gurin, G., 89
Gustavsen, G. A., 128, 131
Guttentag, M., 69

Hackman, J. R., 3, 45, 47, 49, 50, 59, 67, 88, 89, 93, 94, 99, 115, 116, 117, 118
Haimann, T., 38
Hakel, M. D., 44
Hall, D. T., 10, 17
Hall, R. H., 122
Hammer, W. C., 27
Hardin, E., 89
Heiman, G. W., 28
Hellreigel, D., 108
Hemphill, J. K., 2
Heneman, H. G., 21, 29, 36, 89
Herrick, N., 3, 36
Herzberg, F., 23, 43, 44, 45, 131
Hickson, D. J., 24, 122
Higgin, G. W., 42
Hilles, R., 68
Hinrichs, J. R., 44
Hinton, B. L., 44
Hoffman, J., 40
Holly, W. H., 68
Homans, G., 46
Horne, J. H., 2
House, R. J., 3, 21, 44, 121
Hulin, C. L., 41, 42, 44, 63, 82, 83-85
Hunt, R. G., 106, 121

Jablonsky, S. F., 28
Jacox, A., 59
James, L. R., 108
Jasinski, F. J., 40
Jeanneret, P. R., 65, 73
Jenkins, D., 45, 130, 131, 136, 137
Johannesson, R. E., 108
Johnston, W. B., 45
Jones, A. P., 108

Kagno, M., 68
Kahn, R., 121
Kast, F. E., 107
Katz, D., 9, 121
Katzell, R. A., 84
Kaufman, S., 49, 59, 94
Kay, B. R., 2
Keller, R. T., 49, 67
Kelly, J., 2
Kendall, L. M., 63, 84
Kennedy, E. M., 35
Kennedy, J. E., 84
Khandwalla, P. N., 108
Kilbridge, M. D., 42, 84
King, N. A., 44
Knerr, C. S., 62
Koch, J. L., 128, 130, 135

Koch, S., 21
Koeppel, J., 62
Korman, A. K., 2, 26
Kornhauser, A. W., 40, 84
Kraft, W. P., 45
Kreitner, R., 27
Kubany, A. J., 2
Kühne, R. J., 128, 130, 131

Landsberger, H. A., 2
Latham, G. P., 28, 62
Laufer, A. C., 70, 72, 96
Lawler, E. E., III, 2, 12, 18, 20, 23, 40, 47, 49, 59, 60, 67, 69, 88, 94, 98, 115, 116, 117, 118
Lawrence, P. R., 38, 45, 46, 47, 59, 83, 84, 112, 114
Leavitt, H. J., 114
Lenski, G., 85
Lesieur, F. G., 136
Levitan, S. A., 45
Lichtman, C. M., 121
Likert, R., 40
Lirtzman, S. I., 121
Litterer, J. A., 15
Locke, E. A., 44, 62
Lorsch, J. W., 112, 114
Lupton, T., 2
Luthans, F., 27, 45

McCormick, E. J., 65, 66, 73, 74, 97
McEachern, A. W., 121
McFarland, D. E., 38
McGregor, D. M., 40
MacKinney, A. C., 42
Macy, B. A., 36, 69
March, J. G., 111
Martin, N. H., 2
Maslow, A., 9-10, 88
Mason, W. S., 121
Mausner, B., 44
Mawhinney, T. C., 28
Mecham, R. C., 65, 73
Miclette, A. L., 40
Mileti, D. S., 24
Mills, C. W., 37
Mintzberg, H., 2
Mirels, H. L., 86
Miri, J., 131
Mirvis, P. H., 36, 69
Mischkind, L. A., 44
Mitchell, T. R., 21, 49, 60
Morse, J. J., 112
Morsh, J. E., 66
Mowday, R. T., 60, 88

Munsterberg, H., 40
Murray, H., 42
Myers, M. S., 45

Nadler, G., 42
Nemiroff, P. M., 117, 118
Nilsson, S., 2
Nord, W. R., 28
Nougiam, K. E., 10, 17

Oldham, G. R., 49, 50, 67, 88, 89, 99
O'Neill, H. E., 2, 84
Opsahl, R. L., 12
Organ, D. W., 23
Orife, J. N., 45

Parke, E. L., 45
Parker, S. R., 36
Parker, T. C., 84
Partridge, B. E., 68
Paul, W. J., Jr., 45, 131
Pearce, J. L., 49, 99
Perrow, C., 106, 109, 111
Peterson, R. B., 133, 135, 139
Pfeffer, J., 60
Pheysey, D. C., 24, 122
Pierce, J. L., 49, 59, 117, 118, 120
Plasha, F., 45
Pollock, A. B., 42
Ponder, Q. D., 2
Porter, L. W., 2, 18, 23, 49, 88, 115,
     116, 117, 118
Prasad, S. B., 128
Prien, E. P., 65
Pritchard, R. D., 2, 18
Puckett, E. S., 136
Pugh, D. S., 24, 122

Quinn, R., 121

Rafalka, E., 45
Reif, H. G., 89
Reif, W. E., 45
Rhode, J. G., 69
Rice, A. K., 42, 46
Rizzo, J. R., 121
Roach, D. E., 2
Robertson, K. B., 45, 131
Robey, D., 88
Robinson, J., 89
Robinson, R. D., 131
Ronan, W. W., 65
Rose, G. L., 92
Rosenthal, R., 121

Rosenzweig, J. E., 107
Rousseau, D. M., 119, 120
Ruch, F. L., 24
Ruch, W. W., 24
Rush, H. M. F., 43, 45

Salancik, G. R., 60
Schappe, R. H., 45
Schein, E. H., 64
Schmidt, F. L., 21
Schneider, B., 23
Schregle, J., 131
Schuler, R. S., 120, 121
Schwab, D. P., 21, 23, 27, 49, 59
Scott, W. E., 13, 28
Scott, W. G., 38
Shapiro, H. J., 38
Shaw, M. E., 15
Sheppard, H. L., 3, 36
Simon, H. A., 111
Simonds, R. H., 45
Simpkins, E., 85
Sims, H. P., Jr., 49, 67, 87, 88, 98, 99
Sirota, D., 45
Slocum, J. W., 108
Smith, M. A., 36
Smith, P. C., 44, 63, 85, 86
Snoeck, J., 121
Snyderman, B., 44
Spray, S. L., 2
Stalker, G. M., 108, 109, 114
Starke, F. A., 21
Staw, B. M., 60
Steers, R. M., 2, 60
Stewart, P. A., 42
Stewart, R., 2
Stinchcombe, A. L., 114
Stone, E. F., 49, 85, 86, 88, 93
Storey, R. G., 112
Streuning, E. L., 69
Suchman, E. A., 69
Suttle, J. L., 20, 98
Szilagyi, A. D., 49, 67, 87, 88, 98, 99

Tagiuri, R., 108
Tausky, C., 45
Taylor, F. W., 38, 39, 40, 50
Tella, A., 12
Tennenbaum, A., 2
Tharp, R. G., 28
Thomason, G. F., 2
Thompson, J. D., 106, 119
Tiffin, J., 65
Tilgher, A., 37
Tomlinson, J. W. C., 2

Tosi, H., 112
Trist, E. L., 42, 45
Trumbull, R., 97
Terkel, S., 81
Turner, A. N., 38, 40, 45, 46, 47, 59, 83, 84

Udy, S., 114
Umstot, D. D., 49, 60

Valfer, E. S., 42
VanSell, M., 121
Vroom, V. H., 2, 12, 18, 89

Wahba, M. A., 10, 21, 38
Walker, C. R., 40, 42
Wallace, M., 49
Walton, R. E., 3, 36, 45, 138, 139, 140
Wanous, J. P., 49, 88
Weber, M., 13, 85

Weed, E. D., 45
Weick, K. E., 18
Werling, R., 40, 42
Wernimont, P. F., 42
Wetzel, R. J., 28
Wharton, D., 42
Whyte, W. F., 15, 40, 84
Wigdor, L., 44
Wijting, J. P., 85, 86
Williams, K. L., 45
Williams, R. E., 2
Wolfe, D., 121
Wolfson, A. D., 45
Wollack, S., 85, 86
Woodward, J., 114, 119

Yeager, S., 68, 78
Young, W. M., 68
Yukl, G. A., 28, 62

Zedeck, S., 83

SUBJECT INDEX

Ability, 23-25
Achieved status, 15
Activity analysis, 71
Age, 89, 92, 96
Alienation, 84
Anthropometry, 95
Aptitude, 23-25
Ascribed status, 15
Associated Task Attributes, 47
Altas Copco, 134, 135

Behavior, and task attributes, 46
Behavior modification, 27-28
Biorhythms, 97
Bureaucratic organization, 110-11, 117

Codetermination, 128, 130
Commission of European Communities, 130
Congruence, 115-19
Contingency theories, 107
Cultural factors and work, 82

Donnelly Mirrors, 136-37

Educational level, 94
Employee needs, 9-17
Employee participation, 128, 129, 132

Endurance, 96
Energy expenditure, 13, 97
Exercise, 96
Expectancy theory, 18-19

Fatigue, 97-98
Flexitime, 68, 69
Flow process chart, 70

General Foods, 137-38
General Motors, 134
German Codetermination Act, 128

Higher-order need strength, 87-89, 90-91, 117

Industrial psychology, 40
Industrial Revolution, 38
Instrumentality, 20-21
Integration, 84

Job analysis, 65, 72-73
Job Characteristic Inventory, 67
Job content, 59-60
Job Descriptive Index, 63
Job design, history of, 38-41
Job Diagnostic Survey, 67
Job enlargement, 41-43, 44, 45
Job enrichment, 43-45, 128

Job inventory, 65, 66
Job loading, 43
Job perception, 59–60, 67, 93–95
Job performance, measurement of, 25–27; and motivation, 17–21; and nonmotivational factors, 23–25
Job redesign, and employee needs, 9–17; experiments in, 130–39; guidelines for, 139–40; method of, 62–70; and motivation, 22; need for, 63; strategy for, 76; techniques for, 70–75
Job redesign task force, 64–65, 67, 68
Job routinization, 40–41

Knowledge technology, 122

Learning theory, 27–29

McCormick and Company, 136
Management, early theories of, 107; defined, 1–3; role of in job redesign, 64, 139; as a science, 38–39
Materials technology, 122
Mechanistic organization, 108, 109, 111–12
Motion study, 70–72
Motivation, and job performance, 17–21; sources of, 21–23. *See also* Employee needs
Multiple management, 136

Needs, 9–11, 87–89, 90–91
Negative income tax, 12
Neuromuscular factors, 96
Norway, Working Environment Act of, 128

Operation analysis, 71
Operations technology, 122
Organic organization, 108–9
Organizational design, 108–19

Perception of job, 59–60, 67, 93–95
Physiology, 95–98
Position Analysis Questionnaire, 73–75
Process analysis, 70–71
Proctor & Gamble, 137
Protestant work ethic, 13, 37, 84, 85–87

Questor Corporation, 136

Race, 89, 92
Reinforcement theory, 27–29
Religion, and work, 37
Requisite Task Attributes, 47
Role ambiguity, 121
Role conflict, 121
Role perceptions, 24, 25
Routinization, 40–41

Scanlon Plan, 136–37
Sensory-motor tasks, 96
Sex, 89, 92, 96
Situational factors, 98–101
Skandia Insurance Company, 132, 134
Skill, 23–25
Social interaction, 14–15
Social science, and management, 2
Spalding, 136
Status, 15
Strength, 96
Sweden, 131–35

Task attributes, 45–50, 60, 67–68, 82
Task-organization fit, 115–19, 120
Technology, 24, 25, 119–22, 139
Therbligs, 71, 72
Time study, 72
Total systems approach, 137

Urbanization, 83–85

Valence, 19–20
Voluntarism, 132
Volvo, 132, 134

Wages, 12–13
Women, 89
Work, concept of, 36–37. *See also* Job perception, Job performance, Protestant work ethic
Workers' physical characteristics, 95–98
Worker participation, 128, 129, 130
Working Environment Act, 127–28
Work outcomes, 11–17, 20
Works councils, 130

Yale Job Inventory, 67